designing with
simplicity

Redefining Clean with the Artists of Autumn Leaves

Lisa Russo
Debbie Crouse
Jennifer McGuire
Renee Camacho
Kristina Nicolai-White
Ruth Giauque
Tracy Kyle
Cathy Blackstone
Jackie Bonette
Jennifer Bester
Desiree McClellan
Stacy McFadden
Nia Reddy
Julie van Oosten

table of contents

simplicity

It used to be about happy summer days filled with adventure, no shoes and sneaking ice cream straight from the carton. These days **simplicity** is more about happy summer days filled with driving kids to their adventures, low-heeled shoes and waiting until everyone else is asleep so you don't have to sneak the ice cream. With all of life's complexities, it's high time to bring a little simplicity to scrapbooking. What exactly is simplicity? It may be easier to say what it is not: It's not simplistic. It's not technique free. It's not completing forty layouts in one evening. It may not even be easy, and it's definitely not boring. Anne Geddes said, "The hardest thing in photography is to create a simple image." When you have a simpler or cleaner design, the individual elements say more and become more important.
The new clean is like feng shui for your scrapbook. Take all of the beautiful elements and new techniques you love, distill them to their essence and put it all together with a beautiful clean line. Add the latest design trends and it works together to highlight and complement your most amazing photos.
It's time to break out the ice cream.
Pull up your favorite chair and allow us to introduce you to the new clean.

Sophisticated. The new clean meets Madison Avenue for a chic, graphic and oh-so-hot look. With clean lines, interesting type treatments and stand-alone photography, it can't help but sell. Our artists reflect this graphic influence in their projects for a show-stopping trend. The minimalist look is sure to be a favorite for special occasion photographs, nature photography and portraits. Coco Chanel said, "Elegance is refusal." Refusing clutter while going for a graphic look gives you layouts that are pure sophistication.

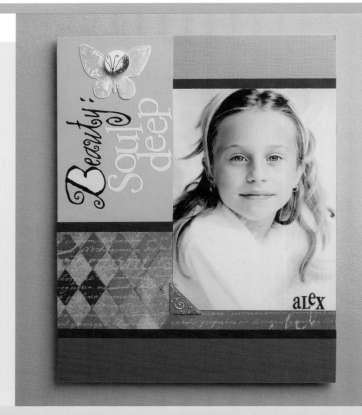

Soul Deep
BY JACKIE

THE PROCESS: Color block background with cardstock and patterned paper. Stamp butterfly in green ink onto white cardstock and trim around image. Stamp butterfly in black ink onto white cardstock and circle punch part of the image. Attach the black stamped circle with a pop dot onto the green butterfly, matching up the two images.

Ryan
BY DESIREE

THE PROCESS: Color block two 8 1/2" X 11" pages with cardstock. Print arrow on vellum and cut out. Attach photo and white journaling block with brads.

Pasta
Gift Set
BY LISA

THE PROCESS: Using a graphic-design program, create personalized labels and adhere to various gift items. To make the tone-on-tone background, fill text boxes with beige and set background text to a tint of the same shade.

Some
Like It Hot
BY DESIREE

THE PROCESS: Color block background with cardstock. Enlarge photo, print on white textured cardstock and use as a background for the right-hand page. Cut an extra strip from a photo and place below the title. Hide journaling behind the title and main photo. Hand cut "HOT" to complete the title.

Just Be You

BY DESIREE

THE PROCESS:
In a photo-editing program, create strips of color. Add text in a complementary color. Print on white cardstock along with the title. Trim 1/2" off all sides. Place four 8 1/2" x 11" sheets behind printed cardstock so just a small strip shows. Add mini circles to journaling strips.

Goofball Ahead

BY DESIREE

THE PROCESS:
Print title ("Warning") onto patterned paper. Place striped paper behind a half circle cut into the right edge. Line up three photos, placing the top of one photo under the cut out circle. Adhere arrow over photos and embellish with brads. Slip journaling under arrow.

Family
BY NIA

THE PROCESS:
Punch 1/8" circles from shades of black, gray and white cardstock to get a variegated effect that matches the font color. Frame printed paper and tie with ribbon.

Security} •

Togetherness} •

Love} ♥

Tenderness} •

are} •

what} •

make} •

a} •

family
Jon · Crystal · Dillan

Husband & Wife
BY TRACY

THE PROCESS:
Adhere photos inside a negative transparency. Mat white cardstock on black. Attach photo and transparency strip at an angle. Add embossed vellum to each side and add strips of black cardstock to the top and bottom. Paint wooden letter and coat with gloss.

2 simply hip

These aren't your Mom's gold tone curtains, tweed couch, or olive green fridge. No sir, this is a fresh blast from the past. It's Simply Hip. Combine colors so yummy you want to reach out and lick them, and graphics like swishes, swirls and polka dots for a fabu-liciously clean look. Where was this trend when orange plaid bellbottoms were in style?

Flower Child Savannah
BY DESIREE

THE PROCESS:
Print title directly on the background. Cut cardstock, patterned paper and vellum in coordinating waves, then adhere so the edges match up. Add main photo so the bottom right corner is under the vellum. Cut flowers from coordinating cardstock and use a circle and buttons for the centers.

Can You Dig Him?
BY DESIREE

THE PROCESS:
Create title and patterned paper on the computer. Print on white paper. Round the corners of the title blocks, patterned paper and photo. Add rivets to the four corners, then tie with leather cord.

779 DON'T LET WEEDS GROW AROUND YOUR DREAMS.

-the complete life's little instruction book-

Become whatever you want to become. Dream high. Dream big. Weed out the negativity constantly so those dreams can flourish. Accomplish whatever you dream to accomplish. Become anything you want to be.

January 2004

Don't Let Weeds Grow
BY RENEE

THE PROCESS: Lightly draw simple patterns (circles, flowers, wavy lines) onto background cardstock, then use an anywhere punch in various sizes to punch along the penciled lines. Erase lines, and back the holes with coordinating cardstock. Sew through the punched elements, adding dimension and texture.

Always Keilah
BY NIA

THE PROCESS: Print title strip on white paper. Print title again on patterned paper and in a large, bold type, allowing some of the words to go off of the page. Use mini paperclips to attach embellishments.

Spirit
BY TRACY

THE PROCESS:
Draw a flowing line on cardstock and cut out. Add journaling and circles to line. Print title on a transparency and attach over printed vellum.

Splash
BY STACY

THE PROCESS: Crop photo into a polygon shape. Cut and mat smaller polygons and an arrow. Print title and stars in outline style in reverse (mirror image) onto the backside of a transparency. Paint with white acrylic paint, then apply a coat of Diamond Glaze over the top to prevent cracking.

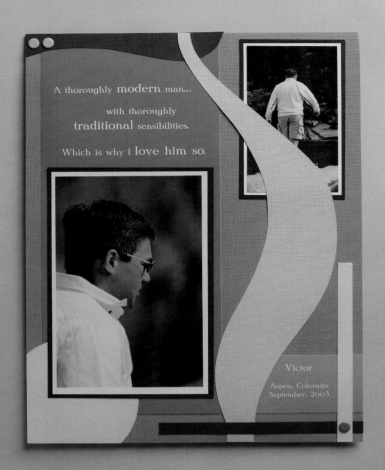

Modern Man
BY LISA

THE PROCESS: Create pink and orange text boxes, then add white text. Print on semi-gloss paper. Cut shapes using a paper trimmer, circle cutter and an X-Acto knife. Mount shapes, text blocks and photos to background cardstock and add brightly-colored snaps or eyelets.

Speedy Little Audrey
BY JENNIFER

THE PROCESS: Create a circular title with Microsoft® WordArt. Enlarge and print a photo, then cut one side in a curve.

Journal
BY TRACY

THE PROCESS:
Cut circles from cardstock and attach to page. Dry emboss circles from the back. Attach painted wooden letters for the title.

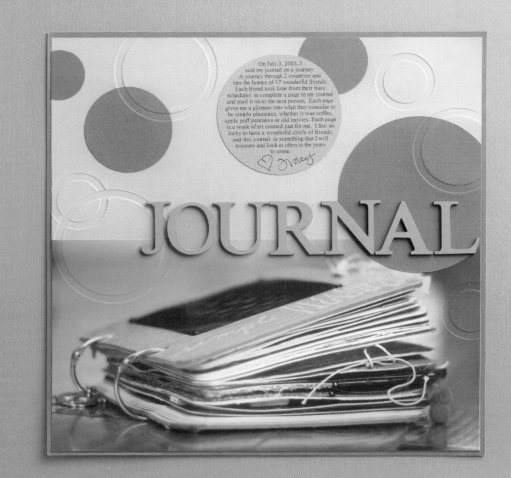

When Did I Grow Up?
BY TRACY

THE PROCESS:
Cut the line designs from cardstock. Layer on background and add wooden flowers.

Stitched
Card Set
BY CATHY

THE PROCESS:
For *Hello* cards,
stitch down one side
of a card, including a
sentiment matted on a
circle. For the *Hi* card,
zigzag stitch a white
rectangle to the front
of a card. Add a small
matted sentiment.

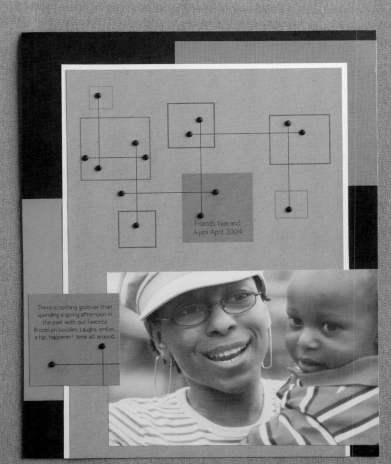

Friends
BY NIA

THE PROCESS:
Use text boxes and
the line tool in
Microsoft® Word to
create the pattern
at the top of the
page. Fill the main
title box and leave
the others open.
Add mini brads to
the end of each line.

Shabby (sha-bee) n: something that has been aged or made imperfect by means of distressing, rumpling, tearing, teasing, smashing, darkening, fading and painting.

Verb: to shab: the act of shab-i-fy-ing a project or object. Often done with acrylic paints, metallic rub-ons, sandpaper, walnut ink, fabric paper, whitewash and ribbon to name a few. To redefine shabby, use distressed embellishments and a faded color palette, then streamline and de-clutter for a clean look that's a little bit lived in.

Tickled Pink
BY DEBBIE

THE PROCESS: Print sentiment, "We are tickled pink!" on a mini tag. Tie tag to feather with thread. Rubber stamp on feather and attach to card with ribbon. Fill clear box with loose feathers. Lightly tape box closed.

6
BY TRACY

THE PROCESS: Cut paper and vellum into strips. Lightly sand edges and adhere to cardstock. Stamp image over the top using paint as the ink. Tie ribbon to metal number and attach to page. Cut bubble letters into various shapes to use for the title.

Lilli

BY LISA

THE PROCESS: Create background with strips of patterned paper. Print text in pink onto vellum and emboss with clear embossing powder immediately after removing from printer. Tear one edge, shade with chalks and attach with snaps. Heat emboss the metal on the vellum tag, then run ribbon through the hole and over the top of the page.

Just a Little Guidance

BY LISA

THE PROCESS: Create background with patterned paper and stamped images. Print and stamp title on blue cardstock, then tear, ink, and mount over ruler paper. Add photo turn, photo corner and brad for embellishment.

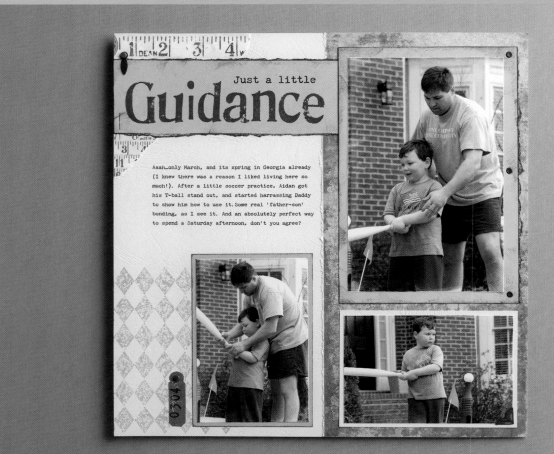

Age 8
BY JENNIFER

THE PROCESS: Cut various patterned and textured papers into large diamonds, mat on white cardstock and rub the edges with brown ink. Attach fabric to cardstock background, then add diamonds and paper flowers. On the journaling block, double stamp age and name— once in brown and once in black.

Almost 2
BY NIA

THE PROCESS: Paint metal tin white. Let dry, then lightly sand. Lightly sponge number stencil with pink paint and adhere to tin. Tear patterned paper and roll one edge. Add title strip with copper brads that have been painted with acrylic paint.

princess

YOU ARE THE PRINCESS OF QUITE A LOT. YOU USED TO GET YOUR WAY A LOT MAKING FOR A SOMETIMES IRRITABLE EVENT WHEN YOU DON'T. IT'S NOT THAT WE WANTED YOU TO GET YOUR WAY, BUT SINCE YOU WERE A LITTLE GIRL, YOU WOULD DEMAND THINGS. BEING THE THIRD CHILD WORKED TO YOUR ADVANTAGE AS THIS CAUSED OTHERS TO GIVE IN TO YOUR LITTLE PITIFUL DEMANDS. YOUR BROTHERS WOULD ALMOST AUTOMATICALLY HAND OVER THE TOYS THEY WOULD BE PLAYING WITH UPON HEARING YOUR LITTLE CRIES. THEY COULDN'T STAND IT. AND BRANDON INSTIGATED A LOT OF THIS BY FORCING ZACHARY TO HAND HIS TOYS OVER AS WELL. HE JUST COULD NOT HANDLE LISTENING TO YOU CRY. AS A RESULT, THE TODDLER YEARS WITH YOU HAVE BEEN TUMULTUOUS, WITH MANY UPS AND DOWNS, BUT IN THE END, I THINK WE'VE SURVIVED WITH A PRETTY LITTLE PRINCESS AS A RESULT, WHO ALTHOUGH YOU'RE USED TO GETTING YOUR WAY, YOU JUST DON'T DEMAND IT AS MUCH AS YOU USED TO! YOU'VE LEARNED THAT CRYING DOESN'T ALWAYS GET YOUR WAY IN THE LAND OF THE CAMACHOS!

—JANUARY 2004

Princess BY RENEE

THE PROCESS: Create background from patterned papers and cardstock, and zigzag stitch along seamed lines. Mat photo and age edges with ink, attaching buttons down one side. Cut out letters for title. Trim bottom edge of layout with decorative scissors.

Baby Gabrielle
BY RUTH

THE PROCESS:
Paint book board with acrylic paint, then sand to expose the edges. Add strips of patterned paper with brads, then rough up the edges with sandpaper.

simply shabby
BY STACY

When you think about mixing clean and shabby, it might sound like mixing water and oil, but it's easy to make shabby style work in a clean, simple way. Combine small shabby accents by keeping them close together on a small part of your page. Stitch strips of fabric or weathered paper to a layout, but keep them linear. Isolate shabby pieces by matting them with bold, solid colors. When inking, try a direct ink method rather than a sponge dauber to get a cleaner edge. Try one or two of these ideas and you'll find that shabby really can lend itself to clean, streamlined design.

Family Farm BY KRISTINA

THE PROCESS: Create the background by adding blocks of patterned paper and fabrics to chipboard. Add twill and ribbon to cover the "seams." Embellish layout with tags, buttons, charms, letter stickers and a safety pin. Stamp title on a transparency and attach with a brad backed with ribbon.

4 simply antique

Forget about skeletons in your closet. What could be scarier than the towering stacks of vintage photos lurking in the dark? It's time to take Granny's photos out of the box and make clean-lined creations that keep the focus on the charm of antique photographs. Stacy's uncluttered treatment and unexpected use of baby blue accentuates the soft baby feel of her *Jack* layout. Desiree's use of patterned blocks are reminiscent of vintage linens. Experiment with new colors and patterns for your own twist on the vintage look.

Words Journal
BY JULIE

THE PROCESS: Cover journal with book fabric. Mount words and a photograph onto heavy core card. Sand edges of all black squares to distress and sponge sepia ink on all kraft-colored blocks. Adhere to journal cover.

Lorene Adelle
BY DESIREE

THE PROCESS: Adhere strips of inked paper to background. Add a button cluster at the bottom of the photo. Print title on a transparency and lay over background. Tie ribbon around layout.

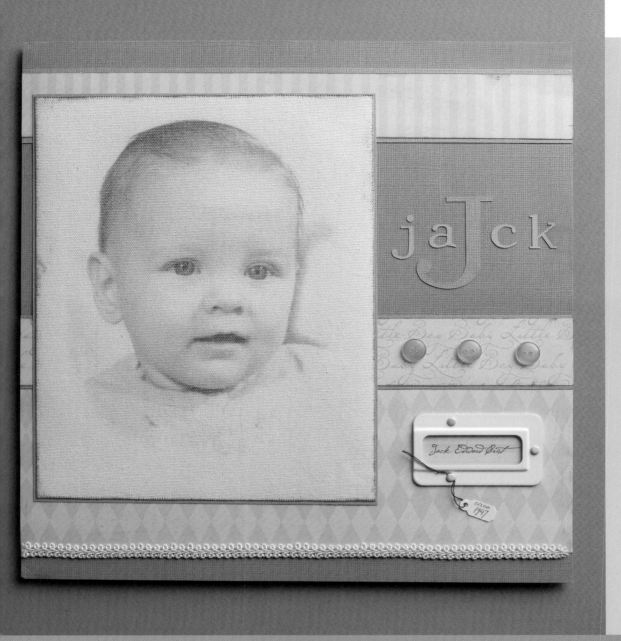

Jack
BY STACY

THE PROCESS:
Print a vintage photo on canvas paper. Cut and mat strips of patterned paper. Arrange on tan cardstock and cover the bottom seam with trim. Print name in reverse and cut out for the title.

Tiny Frame Book
BY JULIE

THE PROCESS: Make a mini book cover and stitch a signature to the inside with waxed linen. Sponge the cover with sepia ink and embellish with small photos and words. Make vintage paper beads by rolling dictionary and sheet music paper around a large needle. Glue the end of the roll to keep it from unraveling and glue a micro eyelet to each end. Thread onto the waxed linen.

Sweet Notes

BY DEBBIE

THE PROCESS: Cover an old mini memo book. Cut a heart-shaped stencil from chipboard. Drip sealing wax into stencil. Using a heat tool or heated spoon, smear edges of heart. Age the edges of the heart with sepia ink. Cut letters from a magazine for the title and make a closure with a button and elastic.

Frieda and the Bunnies

BY LISA

THE PROCESS: Print title directly on photo. Rubber stamp "1931" on background cardstock in matching ink, then lay a printed transparency over the top for a unique background.

Cherish
BY JENNIFER

THE PROCESS: Use a triangle of antique Braille paper for the corner. Lightly rub with brown ink and rubber stamp "cherish" several times with StazOn ink. Embellish with ribbon, trim and charm. Tuck journaling behind the ribbon.

Cowboys
BY TRACY

THE PROCESS: Apply acrylic paint to textured leather paper and wipe off with a cloth, leaving paint in the crevices. Stitch papers together to create background and attach photo with photo flips. Rub paint onto stencils, let dry and lightly sand.

5 simply collage

Sometimes more really is more, but it's time to put the collage movement to the test and take what was once more and make it less. It's the simplicity challenge. Take the feel and style of collage and distill it to a grouping, a tag or even just an impression of collage. It's in the layering of the papers, the gathering of the elements and the tying it all together that makes it simply collaged.

True Friend
BY CATHY

THE PROCESS:
Assemble mini collages on various sizes of metal-rimmed tags to make the page accents.

Mischievous
BY RENEE

THE PROCESS:
Layer several patterned papers onto a black background. Cut the edges of floral paper for added texture. Machine stitch along the bottom of the ledger paper and add stencils, buttons and "M" accents.

Me & My Girls
BY KRISTINA

THE PROCESS:
Attach torn strips of fabric to chipboard. For the corner piece, paint a metal frame, then cut in half. Add velvet ribbon and an enamel plate over the top.

Remember When Card
BY DEBBIE

THE PROCESS:
Layer photos, paper, ephemera and tags onto a square of corrugated cardboard. Secure pieces with a rubber band.

simply secrets

It's almost impossible to keep a secret, and these girls don't intend to try. They have flipped their flaps, come unhinged and boxed their feelings all in an attempt to show how enchanting secrets can be. Snoop inside Kristina's *Ariana at Kindergarten* box to discover secret hiding places and unexpected treasures. Uncover Ruth's passion for secrets as you peek inside her *Chocolate book*. This little book is full of envelopes in all shapes and sizes holding tiny messages and photos. Pilfer a few of our ideas for tucking away your own secrets. We'll never tell...

Chocolate Book
BY RUTH

THE PROCESS: Bind several #10 envelopes by wrapping silver wire around a marker, then threading it through 1/8" holes punched along the short side of the envelopes. Embellish pages with mini envelopes.

Almost Two
BY KRISTINA

THE PROCESS: Arrange patterned papers to create background. Fold three small strips of cardstock in half and adhere one side to the back of the layout to form hinges. Adhere the other side of the strips to a strip of heavy patterned paper to create the flap. Affix patterned paper to the inside of the flap, covering the hinge strips. Arrange library pockets underneath the flap and insert synonym tabs.

INSIDE DETAIL OF LEFT PAGE

A @ K
BY KRISTINA

THE PROCESS:
Cover a small box with patterned papers. Cut three pieces of foam core to fit inside the bottom of the box. Cut out one corner for the decorated tin to sit in. Cover the foam core with patterned paper. Hinge an embellished square of chipboard to the foam board. Attach a ribbon tab to one side of the chipboard.

Groovy Love
BY DESIREE

THE PROCESS:
Cut a scalloped design on the right-hand side of two pieces of cardstock. Print song lyrics onto a white piece of cardstock, which also doubles as a photo mat. Attach photo over the lyrics with brads in the top two corners. Adhere title to only the photo, using brads in the top corners. Lift the title to read the lyrics.

a *groovy* kind of love.

simply secrets
BY RUTH

I love a good secret, and some of my favorite places to keep them are in my scrapbooks, book projects and art journals.

Just think of the possibilities:

✛ windows with sliding doors that move back and forth by the pull of a ribbon

✛ hidden doors that reveal pictures or heartfelt journaling

✛ pockets that hide funny photos, surprising journaling or secret information

✛ coin envelopes with windows cut into them

✛ CD cases full of ephemera and secured to a layout or journal

✛ photos that peek out from behind pop-ups

✛ strings of old-fashioned paper dolls that open to show journaling

✛ glassine envelopes with treasures hidden inside

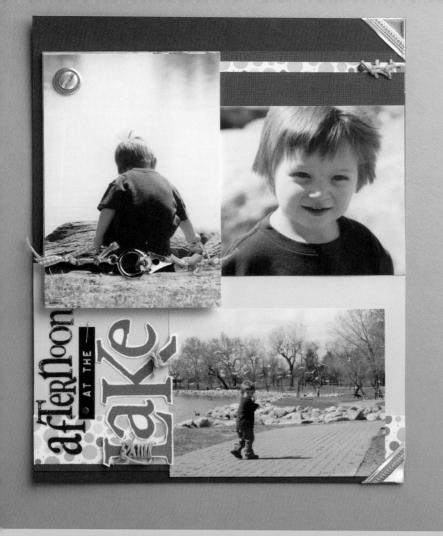

Afternoon at the Lake
BY JACKIE

THE PROCESS:

Gather extra photos and punch a hole in the upper left corner. Journal on 4" x 6" paper and punch the upper corner, as well. Attach the extra photos and journaling to the layout with a screw closure and washer. Hold the photos together with a decorative band made from hemp cording and clothing closures.

Mom's Flowers
BY RENEE

THE PROCESS:

Create background with torn paper sewn to cardstock. Cut slits in the background cardstock slightly larger than the width of the index cards. Sew entire page to a second sheet of cardstock. Add journaling and titles to index cards, then insert into the slits.

Transparencies used to be high tech. Combined with smelly markers and a circa 1960's overhead projector, you had one of the grooviest 6th grade math presentations going. Who would have known way back then that transparencies would be finding their place in our scrapbooks? Flash forward forty years or so and it's time to bust out the transparencies once again. Print your photos on them, paint sew, stamp, cut, layer or even write on them. Clearly, transparencies are the thing, even if you hated 6th grade math.

Snickleritz ... found a sunny spot again.

Sun
BY TRACY

THE PROCESS:
Attach alphabet stickers to a transparency, then brush paint over the top. Let dry, then carefully remove stickers. Attach transparency to page with ribbon.

Flowers BY KRISTINA

THE PROCESS: Press petals between two glass slides and tie with ribbon. Insert slides in a transparency pocket. Cut the front of a string envelope to create another pocket. Tie a magnifying glass to the envelope flap and tuck it into a glassine envelope.

Sing
BY LISA

THE PROCESS:
Color block background and add text and cardstock diamonds. Apply an artistic border to a digital image and print on a transparency. Attach with mini brads.

simply clear

BY TRACY

Whether you choose pre-printed, print some yourself or stamp and paint on them, there are so many different looks you can achieve with transparencies. There is no easier way to add a bit of layered complexity to your page. Simple applications such as using transparencies for journaling or titles can be done with your printer, stickers or by hand. Experiment with color using ink or paint. Try printing photos on them, then layering over other page elements. It is clear that transparencies can fit into any style of scrapbook page effectively.

Heartbeat
BY JENNIFER

THE PROCESS: Print title and journaling onto a transparency. As soon as it is done printing, immediately shake red embossing powder on the title and gently heat to emboss. Add flowers and stamped fabric to background. Sew transparency over the top.

My little dog...
a heartbeat at my feet.

Edith Wharton

Transparency Booklet BY TRACY

THE PROCESS: Cut a transparency to fit inside a library pocket. Apply paint to the back of the transparency, let dry, then attach a photo and rub-on words to the front. Fold strips of metal tape over the edges of the transparency for stability. Staple a folded piece of patterned paper to the top. Accordion fold a strip of cardstock, attach library pockets and tie closed with ribbon.

Cards
BY CATHY

THE PROCESS:
Fold cardstock into thirds and cut a window in one corner. Stitch a printed transparency behind the window. Add fabric or a sticker behind the transparency. Thread ribbon through an eyelet to close.

Faces of You
BY DESIREE

THE PROCESS:
Print title on 8"-wide cardstock, then add two rows of photos, being sure to leave a space for journaling. Print journaling on a transparency and adhere to cardstock. Create six text boxes, changing the fill color to blue and text to white. Arrange boxes so the text will be directly over the photos, then print onto a transparency. With brads, attach a blank transparency to the back of the printed one, then slide in the cardstock.

In Your Eyes
BY RENEE

THE PROCESS:
Print title and journaling using varying font sizes and font types. Use a corner rounder on the edges of journaling. Zigzag stitch vellum to cardstock background.

Nicholas
BY STACY

THE PROCESS:
Print name in different fonts onto a transparency and print journaling on a small transparency. On a gray strip, randomly arrange circles and small cardstock strips. Arrange transparencies and embellished strip on black cardstock, laying the journaling over a cut out "N" and hiding the seam of transparency under the gray strip.

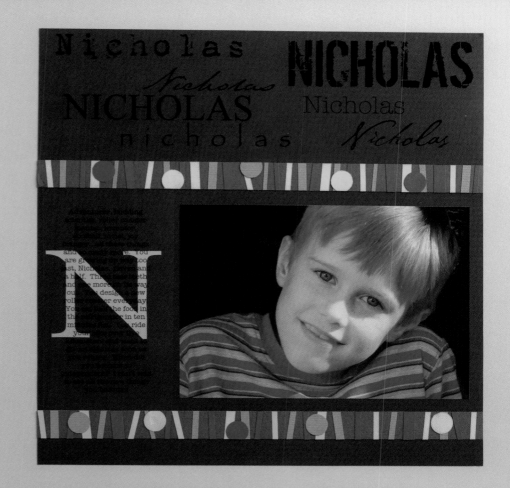

Lot #291
BY DEBBIE

THE PROCESS:
Preserve items from a special location in a glass bottle, such as items from a house lot. Add sawdust first, then add wire, wood, nails, washers and cardboard. Reduce floor plans, roll them up and insert in the bottle. Seal the cork with wax, and then add ribbons and a tag.

simply silly

8

Life is short. It's easy to focus on the day-to-day grind and forget to stand back every once in a while and realize, "Gosh, my family is full of weirdos." It's the humor in the mix that makes it all palatable. From funny photos of cute little bottoms to finding the fun in a traffic jam and journaling about it, it's time to lighten up. These artists added a dash of humor to their layouts and in the process captured something of what it means to be alive.

Daddy...Mommy Has a Baby
BY CATHY

THE PROCESS:
Create a blocked, monochromatic background by adhering squares and rectangles from a darker shade of brown to a lighter brown cardstock. Hand stitch a railroad-like design, then randomly add eyelets.

Bop-It
BY NIA

THE PROCESS:
Fill a text box with gray and change text to white. Choose a few words to print in green, red and yellow. Print on white paper. Add diagonal strips of cardstock and add conchos where the strips overlap.

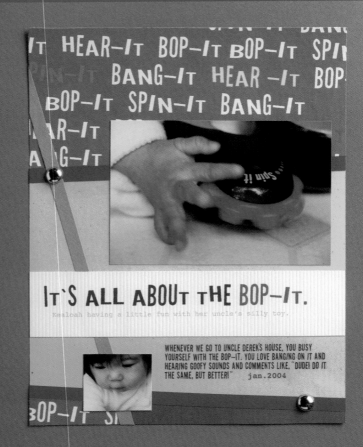

IT'S ALL ABOUT THE BOP-IT.

Kealoah having a little fun with her uncle's silly toy.

WHENEVER WE GO TO UNCLE DEREK'S HOUSE, YOU BUSY YOURSELF WITH THE BOP-IT. YOU LOVE BANGING ON IT AND HEARING GOOFY SOUNDS AND COMMENTS LIKE, "DUDE! DO IT THE SAME, BUT BETTER!" jan.2004

Little Behind
BY DEBBIE

THE PROCESS:
Print a photo onto cardstock and add text over the photo. Score and fold. Store cards in an envelope embellished with a custom label and ribbon.

IDEA TO NOTE:
The captions include: "But, but...," "You crack me up," "Bummer," "We were just talking about you," "No ifs, ands or buts about it" and "I'm a little behind."

True Story DVD Case
BY NIA

THE PROCESS:
Use an old CD or DVD case to hold memories. Decorate the front and inside cover. Lift out the plastic from the back cover and place patterned paper underneath. Decorate an old CD with words, tags and rubber stamps.

simply silly

BY LISA

Wouldn't it be wonderful if you could leave your audience with a big smile when they flip through your scrapbooks? You can! Start by adding a few fun titles, some silly photos and clever journaling. Did your child say something completely outrageous? Don't sugarcoat it when you journal; quote him exactly. Have a photo that just makes you burst out laughing? Use it on a page right now. If you have neither a funny story nor photo, but just want to make your reader smile, invent a funny title using your inherent wit (yes, we all have some). If all else fails, go with color. Bright colors, wacky page design or unique color combinations can help big time in the silly department. Are we having fun yet?

Littlest Bottom

BY JENNIFER

THE PROCESS:

Cut a curve on one side of patterned paper and adhere over blue cardstock. Line up small embellished circles along the curved edge. Design journaling to follow the curve.

New Zealand
Traffic Jam

ON THE ROAD FROM QUEENSTOWN TO WANAKA.

New Zealand Traffic Jam

BY STACY

THE PROCESS: Print title in reverse and cut out. Add letter stickers for subtitle. Embellish with small circles and cardstock strips. Adhere smaller photo with pop dots.

Hair Salad

BY LISA

THE PROCESS: Create the title by altering the size, location, spacing and color of the letters. For the green strips, create text boxes with a solid color fill and set text color to white.

HAIR salad
{OR IS IT ICE CREAM?}

| EGG PLANT | TURNIP | TOMATO | SWEET BASIL | CAULIFLOWER |

You were a baldy baby - it took a LONG time for your hair to grow in. But ever since it did, this is what you look like - every morning. The combination of thick hair, lots of it, and erratically-placed cowlicks results in this standing-up mess on top of your head.

Kinda ruins the early-morning photo ops, doesn't it? (Well, except for this one time...)

Hair Salad.

That's what you call it. You run into the bathroom "Look, hair salad, mommy!" Oh yeah, most definitely hair salad. Tossed.

Most kids need to brush their teeth in the morning. We call it 'teeth and hair,' since I have to bring out the taming tools: a comb and a spray bottle of water. You brush your teeth, I tame the salad. Haircuts don't make much of a difference, either - for some reason they simply result in more of a field greens salad, as opposed to your regular tossed variety.

Oh, wait - you just informed me that it will heretofore be known as:

Ice Cream Sundae Hair.

Guess we know what you're thinking about, don't we? Ok, Ice Cream Sundae hair it is.

| ARTICHOKE | RADISH | ONION | CARROT |

simply colorful

Never mind a splash of color, it's time to bathe yourself in unadulterated, knock-your-socks-off hues. Make it saturated, make it muted, tease with color or hit somebody over the head with it. Spice it up and make it colorful! Chill with the cool colors of Debbie's monochromatic *Bluz card* or lap up the lush lines in Jennifer's *Vivid Color* layout. Vivid not your thing? Try the same palette in a more subdued tone like Kristina's *Harmony*. These clean-lined projects allow the color to steal the show. Why not venture out and pick a new palette for your own projects?

More Than I Ever Imagined
BY CATHY

THE PROCESS:
Cut journaling at random intervals. Poke a trail from the butterfly with a needle. Back the holes in the dark brown background with white cardstock. Ink the edges of the cardstock blocks.

Gift Tag & Box Set
BY JULIE

THE PROCESS:
Attach mini frames to box lid and front. Add letter tiles inside the frames and add words to the sides. Adhere word blocks to tags. Set eyelets in the tags and thread onto a wire loop with jump rings.

My
adorable
sweet
easy
happy
fair
skinned
red
headed
blue
eyed
dreamy
little
Brynn
that
is
growing
up
way
too
fast!

Brynn
BY CATHY

THE PROCESS: Machine stitch blocks of fabric to cream cardstock. Add matted photo and journaling cut into individual pieces. Ink edges of cardstock, then stitch to green background.

Harmony
BY KRISTINA

THE PROCESS:
Adhere papers on background cardstock and secure a printed transparency to layout with a long bar. After adhering the photo, attach photo turns to the right side of the photo. Rubber stamp title on a transparency and attach with brads.

all of my world in harmony.

my 3 kids
good friends
my favorite season
great weekend
at stockhausens
September 2003

TOP 10 REASONS I LOVE MY JOB

10. I GET TO BE CREATIVE.

9. I GET NEW HERO ARTS STAMPS IN MY MAILBOX SEVERAL TIMES A WEEK.

8. I GET TO WORK WITH WONDERFUL PEOPLE.

7. I GET TO TRAVEL ALL OVER THE WORLD TEACHING.

6. I GET TO WEAR MY PAJAMAS TO WORK.

5. I DON'T HAVE TO PAY $1.90/GALLON TO GET TO MY OFFICE.

4. I CAN WORK WITH MY PUPPY ON MY LAP.

3. I HAVE BECOME FRIENDS WITH MY UPS MAN AND FEDEX LADY DUE TO FREQUENT DELIVERIES.

2. I HAVE AN EXCUSE TO TAKE LOTS OF PICTURES.

1. NOTHING IS BETTER THAN THE INSTANT FRIENDS I HAVE MADE...

CATHY & I MET SHORTLY AFTER WE BOTH WON HALL OF FAME. WE HAD AN INSTANT CONNECTION & HAVE BEEN FRIENDS EVER SINCE. I FEEL BLESSED TO BE WORKING WITH HER ON SEVERAL SCRAPBOOKING PROJECTS, ALLOWING US THE PERFECT EXCUSE TO SEE EACH OTHER OFTEN. CATHY IS A CONSTANT REMINDER OF WHY I LOVE MY JOB SO MUCH. • APRIL 2004 •

passion

J & C
BY JENNIFER

THE PROCESS:
Journal on strips of various colored cardstock. Back metal stencils with cardstock, then mat on a coordinating color.

Vivid Color
BY JENNIFER

THE PROCESS:
Create a replica eye chart using several font colors.

S

Audrey

EE

sees the world in such

THE

vivid color. Since having her in my

WORLD

life, I see the world in the same vivid color.

IN VIVID

And what a colorful world it is. Love this girl.

COLOR. J & A.

MARCH04DISNEY

The Blūz
BY DEBBIE

THE PROCESS:
Print text on watercolor paper, eliminating all the "blue" words. Using various shades of blue, paint on card. Varying intensity and tones of the watercolors can make different shades. Stitch around the perimeter of the card.

blūz

I'm so [ ] you [ ] it!
[ ] velvet
print
berry
red roses for a [ ] lady
[ ] a fuse [ ] suede shoes
up baby [ ]
[ ] jeans
singing the [ ] [ ]
[ ] man group
ribbon
(song)
I've got the [ ]
blood
navy [ ] wild [ ] yonder
my [ ] heaven
moon
Moody [ ] [ ]
without you

simply stitched

Look who's traded in their glue sticks for a needle and thread. These girls are just bursting at the seams with ideas that give new purpose to your old sewing machine. See how stitching can add the texture needed to keep a clean-lined layout from becoming a little too plain. Stitching is so fast, easy and fun you'll be tempted to say, "Goodbye glue."

Fleur Card
BY JENNIFER

THE PROCESS:
Stamp a fleur de lis on white cardstock. Scan on computer, increase the size to 4 1/2" and print on scrap paper. Lay on top of an envelope and punch holes around the image with a needle. Do the same on the front of the note card. Rubber stamp on fabric with VersaMark ink and heat emboss with platinum powder.

Cheekwood Architecture
BY RENEE

THE PROCESS:
Print photo onto canvas and attach to watercolor paper background. Print journaling onto tissue paper, then decoupage to watercolor paper. Press cheesecloth into wet decoupage medium, leaving it slightly crumpled. Paint around picture and journaling with white acrylic paint. Hand sew buttons and a border around the photo.

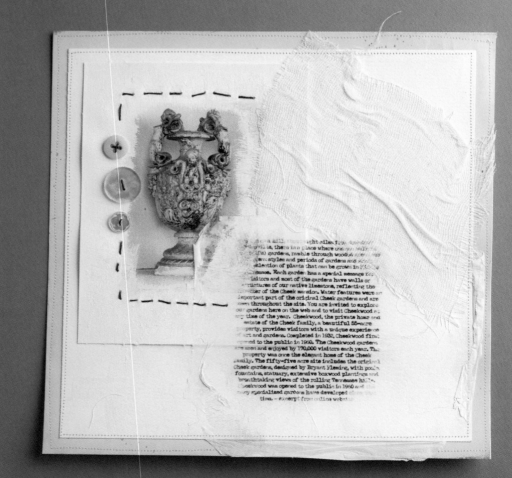

Channing

BY RENEE

THE PROCESS:
Mount patterned paper onto background cardstock. Print journaling, cutting each individual letter and attaching to background. Faintly trace diamond background onto patterned paper, then machine stitch over trace marks.

Loves Me, Loves Me Not

BY DEBBIE

THE PROCESS:
With a straight edge, tear watercolor paper into rectangles (tear two per flower). Machine stitch the paper together onto stem and add a sentiment. Curl the edges and tie a ribbon bow.

Mackenzie

BY JACKIE

THE PROCESS:
Zigzag stitch strips of patterned paper and cardstock to the top of a layout. Add various types of letters for the title.

Hugging

BY CATHY

THE PROCESS:
Straight stitch a line every two inches to form a grid. Add squares and round tags to a few squares.

There is absolutely nothing like seeing the man you are deeply in love with **hugging** the daughter that you adore... nothing.

One Year Old
BY CATHY

THE PROCESS:
Machine stitch several times around cardstock squares and rectangles to create a border. Embellish with photos, buttons, ribbon, etc. Arrange around focal photo that is matted on a scrap of fabric.

Loveable
BY KRISTINA

THE PROCESS:
Cover an 8 1/2" x 11" piece of cardstock with a printed transparency. Adhere two-sided vellum to the lower half of the layout. Machine stitch a strip of fabric to the middle, then add photo and acrylic heart.

simply stamped

This is where the new clean and stamping meet. It's all about clean-lined projects that focus on stamping techniques. Don't miss Tracy's colorful stamped accents for her *Cherish* layout; let Lisa wow you with stamping over photos in her *Roses* layout. Our artists have had a great time cleaning up their act and you will too with these simply amazing stamped projects.

Cherish the Moment
BY TRACY

THE PROCESS:
Using resist ink, rubber stamp pen image onto glossy paper. Stamp over the top with a diamond image and chalk ink. Rub off excess ink. Cut out diamonds and adhere with pop dots. Further embellish layout with strips of patterned paper and rub-ons.

Create
BY RENEE

THE PROCESS:
Paint white acrylic paint over patterned paper, allowing the pattern to slightly show. Stitch painted paper onto kraft-colored cardstock. Rubber stamp rectangular strips and attach to page with various embellishments.

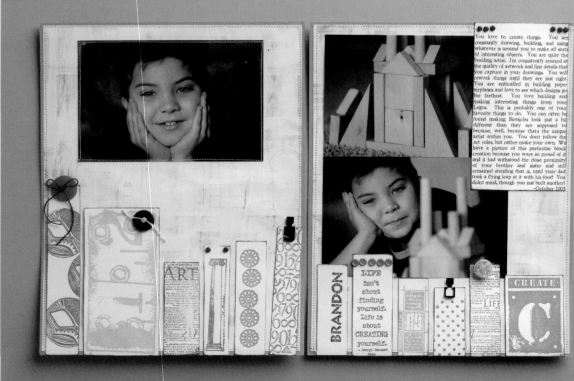

Franny's Playhouse

BY JENNIFER B.

THE PROCESS:
Ink a brayer with VersaMark, and run it over three different colors of textured cardstock. Arrange blocks of cardstock in desired pattern. Add photos, embellishments and journaling printed on vellum.

Giggle

BY NIA

THE PROCESS:
Add text to a photo in a photo-editing program. Ink a rubber stamp with various colors, being sure the stamp is evenly covered (this will result in the color-blended effect). Place stamped letter inside an envelope and tie with ribbon.

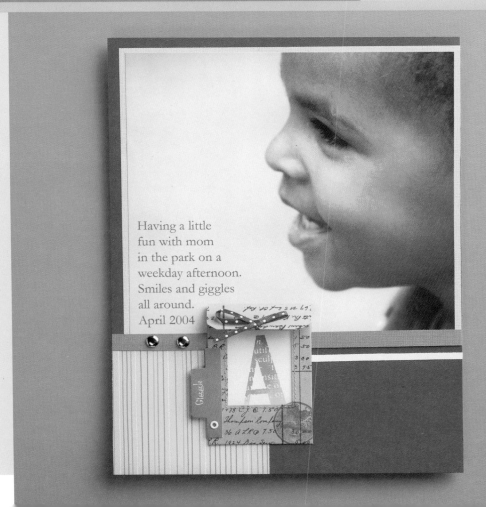

Having a little fun with mom in the park on a weekday afternoon. Smiles and giggles all around. April 2004

Remarkable
BY JENNIFER

THE PROCESS:

Rubber stamp images with VersaMark ink, then apply dry Pearl-Ex with a fine paintbrush for added shine. To make the metal embellishment, wipe VersaMark ink on a cardstock square. Apply several layers of clear embossing enamel. On the final layer, add platinum embossing powder. While still hot, shake in gold Pearl-Ex and press in a rubber stamp until cool.

Roses
BY LISA

THE PROCESS:

Rubber stamp background cardstock with harlequin pattern and the date, then add a small photo to the lower right corner. Stamp swirl image on a transparency and lay over the top. Add torn patterned paper over to the top half. Add title, journaling, photos and brads.

J & C
BY KRISTINA

THE PROCESS:
Cut foam core to an 8"
square and cut a hole in
the lower left corner.
Adhere stamped paper to
the back of the hole. Make
a flap from heavy
patterned paper held on by
two small strips of
cardstock. Cover the front
and back of the foam core
with patterned paper,
cutting away the hole on
the front. Glue a gold
frame inside the hole.
Attach a transparency flap
with hinges. Add a matted
photo to the paper flap.

A Boy and His Boots
BY RUTH

THE PROCESS:
Glue kraft-colored
paper to a 12" square
of mat board. Paint
with cream-colored
acrylic paint,
then sand. Add
stamped title and
stencil number.

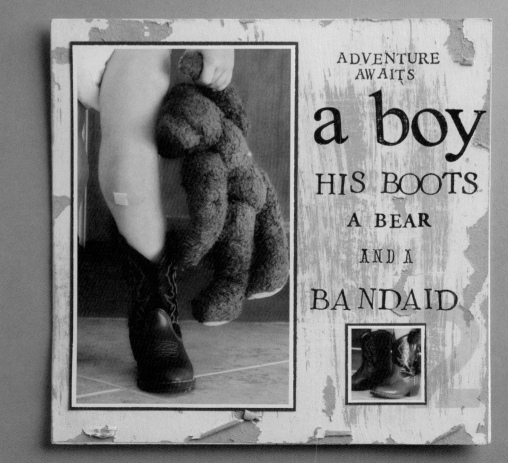

While an itsy bitsy teeny weenie yellow polka dot bikini might not be your thing, here's your big chance to go for **Ms. Junior Petite** with mini books. Petite books and photos are all the rage and it's no small wonder that they have hit the big time. They are cute, portable and don't ride up on you when you run. Grab your beach towel and sun block and try on for size what our artists have done with the mini book.

A Perfect Trip to Boston
BY LISA

THE PROCESS: Adhere together 4" tall strips of cardstock (they can be any length). Fold into an accordion book. Adhere business-card pockets to each "page" to hold photos. Adhere the accordion to the center of a 4-1/4" tall cardstock strip, then trim so it's just long enough to wrap around the book.

a perfect trip to Boston

August 2003

Park Play

BY NIA

THE PROCESS: Cut a front and back cover from patterned paper. Cut cardstock filler pages and add journaling and photos. String pages together with bead chain. Slip book into a paper holder

simply petite
BY JENNIFER B.

I like to work on small projects that can be completed quickly. I've discovered how much I can accomplish when I work on mini albums. Once I pick a format and a color scheme, it's all about the photos and the journaling, and I don't have to hem and haw over the design of every page. I've found that the list of page ideas I keep in my sketchbook can be adapted to a mini-album format. Recently, I have completed mini albums about the nicknames we have given my daughter over the years and a Top 5 Reasons I Love You book for my husband. When it comes to small projects like these, the key is to relax, have fun and enjoy working with a smaller sized page. Once you try them, I guarantee your first album will become the first of many!

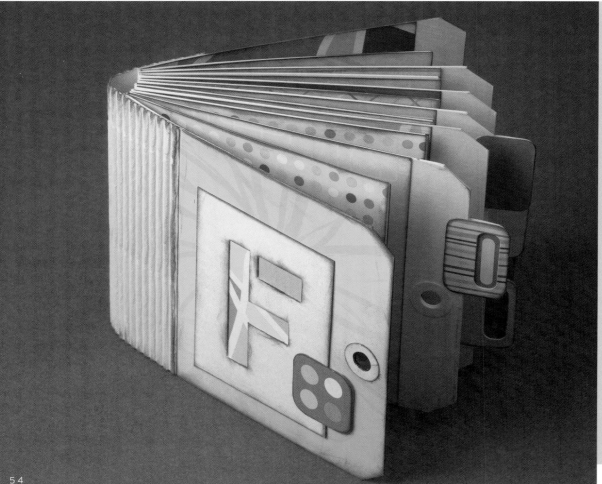

Manila Tag Book
BY JENNIFER B.

THE PROCESS:
Fold large tags up to just below the hole. Starting with pairs of tags, adhere short ends together. Then adhere two pairs together using the longer end until all tags are adhered together. "Bind" with a strip of corrugated paper.

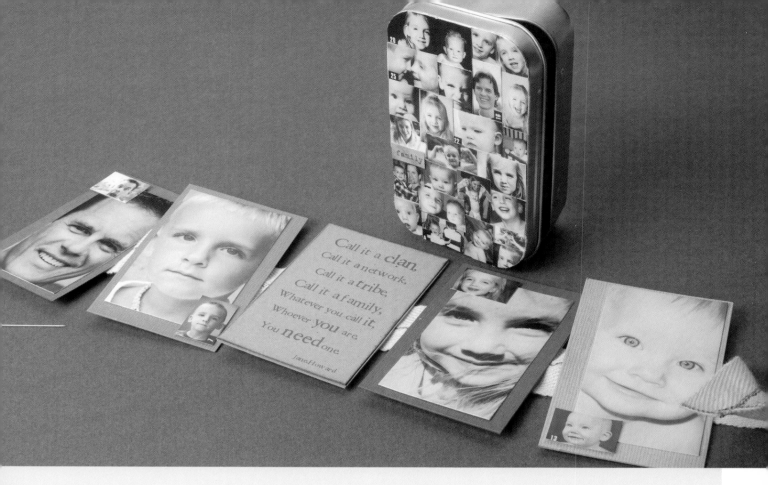

Family Tin BY CATHY

THE PROCESS: Decoupage mini photos to a tin lid. For the mini book, machine stitch cardstock to twill. Add photos over the stitching. Fold up and close with a t-pin. Set eyelets at the top and glue on letters tiles. Mount words onto heavy core card, sand or ink the edges. Bind file dividers and attach a barbed elastic for the closure.

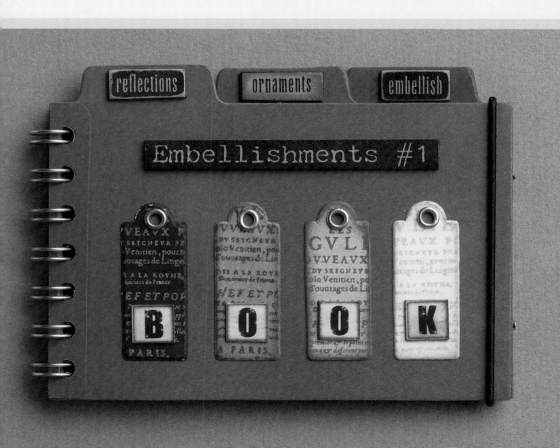

File Divider Book

BY JULIE

THE PROCESS: Rubber stamp text onto small tags using various ink colors. Set eyelets at the top and glue on letters tiles. Mount words onto heavy core card, then sand or ink the edges. Bind file dividers and attach a barbed elastic for the closure.

The School Years

BY TRACY

THE PROCESS: Cut several cardstock squares and round the corners. Use spray adhesive to adhere front and back pages together, and slip twill in between the layers for the binding. Slip fabric strips between the layers of the front and back cover to create a closure. Adhere photos to cardstock pages, putting half of the school years on the front and half on the back.

Pocketbook

BY STACY

THE PROCESS:

Stitch a matted photo to pocket and iron on a title. For the book inside, cut pages about 1/2" smaller than pocket opening. Punch holes along top edge and bind with large jump rings decorated with ribbon.

Happy
Thoughts

BY RUTH

THE PROCESS:
Start with a ready-made
accordian album. Back clear
buttons with cardstock and
stamp large button with script
stamp using StazOn ink. Use
contact sheet photos to
further embellish the cover.

Compendium Book

BY JULIE

THE PROCESS:
Trim paper to desired size, then fold in half. Form pockets on the inside and secure with eyelets. Fill with embellished tags and glassine envelopes filled with mini cards. For the cover, sandwich the title between two glass slides, wrap with copper tape and solder. Fashion a closure with organza ribbon and a silver bead.

Lifetime
BY KRISTINA

THE PROCESS:
Rubber stamp title on patterned paper and label sticker. Construct a matchbook-style book to house journaling.

Watch Fob
BY JULIE

THE PROCESS:
Remove the front of a watch fob and line the inside with dictionary paper. Mount photo and words on heavy core card. Layer over background, then replace top of watch. Finish off with ribbon and a tag.

simply tied

With all the gorgeous ribbons, fibers, elastics and strings available, these artists just couldn't resist tying one on—their pages, of course. See how they used some of their all-time favorite accents to create fun "tied" layouts and projects. Check out the way Nia tied these sensational journaling tags to her *True Style* layout and look how Lisa used string to tie up her amazing *Travel Folio*. Find inspiration galore for new and exciting ways to "tie it up."

Just Be
BY NIA

THE PROCESS:
Use a circle punch and brads to make string and tie closures to attach one photo to the next. Wrap ribbon around a metal-rimmed tag and tuck accents behind.

Green
BY STACY

THE PROCESS:
Create a blue text box and add white journaling. Print onto photo paper. Arrange journaling, green border and orange strip onto white cardstock. Attach eyelets on the edges of the journaling block and photo mat, then tie ribbon through the pairs of eyelets.

THE PROCESS: Cut photos and accent paper into small rectangles, then round the edges. Tie metal-rimmed tags with ribbon and embellish with part of a paint chip.

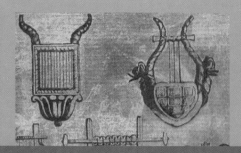

true
STYLE

Aiden you are a true stylin' little man. As soon as I found out I was pregnant with a boy, I spent a day out walking Madison Ave. doing a little shopping for cute, one of a kind outfits for you to wear when you arrived.

Of course as soon as you were born, I had a real live model, so that made shopping even more fun. Although it is not your favorite thing to do (I think you get that from your father) - I love to spend the day going around to all my favorite stores in the city to buy you clothes.

So style on little man...you sure look good to me, and I will never tire of buying you new gear.

They say the CLOTHES make the man. You definitely make the CLOTHES.
— mommy

Gift
BY CATHY

THE PROCESS:
Cut out each letter of "gift" and "dreamt," then mount onto tan strips within the title block. Add knotted ribbon to the centers of silk flowers. String ribbon across the layout and secure with corsage pins. Embellish with accent ribbons.

You have given me a *gift* such as I have never *dreamt* of finding

Carefree Companions
BY JENNIFER

THE PROCESS:
Cut cardstock in angled pieces and adhere over photo. Add photo negative, tying various items in the holes. Use rub-ons for the journaling.

carefree companions

heaven sent

Aspen Travel Folio

BY LISA

THE PROCESS:
To make the flaps, cut a 12" x 12" sheet of dark blue cardstock in half. Trim one side of each half into a modified "V" shape. Cover each side with patterned paper. Trim two 1" strips of dark blue cardstock, score down the middle and attach to the outside edge of each cover piece with copper brads. Fold over and attach the back of each strip to a 12" x 12" sheet of yellow cardstock. For the ties on the front, punch circles from cardstock and attach with eyelets. Wind floss or ribbon to close.

Aspen, Colorado – September, 2003

September, 2003

Sometime during the summer, Dave Lausa asked Vic if he'd like to come up to the Aspen Ruggerfest and play with their travelling team – The Clowns.

Since Vic's never one to turn down a rugby tournament, and I'm never one to turn down a trip to Aspen, off we went!

We decided to fly into Denver rather than Aspen, so we could drive through the mountains. We accidentally took the loooonnnnggg way getting there, but it was SO gorgeous. We went over the mountains – above the tree line. We stopped at the Continental Divide (photo at bottom left).

Aspen itself is SUCH a cool and funky place – full of super-rich people trying to look like they're not (e.g. no makeup and casual clothes). Pretty funny, actually. The shops were interesting, to say the least – a little out of our price range!

We were most amazed by the homes in the area – driving around the foothills, we tried to guess which celebrity lived where. Fun!

Of course we had to take the gondola up to the top of Aspen mountain. Vic and Aidan were much amused by my fear of heights, and kept swinging the dang thing. Thanks, guys!

Up at the top, we went for a hike through the woods, and I shot about 3 rolls of film (no surprise there). It's HARD to hike in that thin air! The trip was a little boring for Aidan overall, but he seemed to enjoy the hiking with Daddy.

On our 3rd day, we ran into our friends Dave and Colleen (nice surprise), and they told us to visit the Maroon Bells. We did just that the next day – SOO cool. They sat at the end of this amazing valley. The leaves were turning, the aspens were vivid yellow. Just gorgeous. You can see them in the photos on the top, and the aspens on the bottom right.

On our 2nd to last day, we visited the Balloon Festival, but got there about 2 hours too late (who knew they had to depart at 6:00 a.m.??). Aidan didn't know the difference – ha!

So that's about it for our trip – aside from a visit to some local caves on the last day (we're not a "sit around" family, I guess!). The Clowns didn't do so well in the tournament, but Vic didn't care – it was just nice to get away as a family and not think about work. Our quaint hotel had a heated pool, so you can guess what Aidan's favorite part was.

I wonder where rugby will take us next??

Travel
BY KRISTINA

THE PROCESS:
Block paper with photos
and patterned paper.
Punch holes on layout, and
thread ribbon and fabric
into the holes, tying some
in the back and some in
the front. Wrap a bit of
fabric around one edge of
the layout and attach with
a brad. Tuck stickers and
printed twill into fabric
strips that have been
tacked down with brads.

My Dog
BY TRACY

THE PROCESS:
Enlarge photo to 8" x 12".
Using text boxes, create title
words, then frame with
book plates. Attach title to
mesh with foam squares,
then tie to mesh with
ribbon. Adhere photo to
layout with foam squares.

Christian
BY RUTH

THE PROCESS: For the "XOXO" party stick, wrap a shish kabob stick with ribbon and glue ends to secure. Add acrylic letters backed with cardstock to the top of the decorated stick. Layer knotted ribbons to create photo frame.

simply tied

BY NIA

Fibers, string, twine and ribbon—all of these can completely change the mood of a layout depending how they're used. Take a layout from humdrum to WOW by adding soft, hand-died silk ribbon or tying a soft fiber across the page. String tags, charms or mini photos from a few different strands of ribbon for a fun page accent. Mix and match different colors and textures to give your page some softness and pizzazz. The truth is, when I am stumped on a page and all else fails, I "tie it up." You're always bound to create something amazing with a little ribbon!

Happily Ever After
BY RUTH

THE PROCESS: Mat photos with colored paper. Embellish with ribbon and trim. Place a mini accordion book in the center square and tie closed with embroidery floss.

Danke Schoen
BY DESIREE

THE PROCESS: Color block the background with various cardstock colors. Print title onto vellum and hand cut a wavy border. Tie ribbon around conchos and secure to a strip of blue cardstock. Print the four journaling blocks and adhere photos to the top.

simply words

Speak to me baby! Look deep into my eyes and say something sweet. Curl my toes... Shock me... I don't care what you say... read me the phone bill... but just SAY SOMETHING!

The right words are like chocolate ice cream on a hot summer day. They can make just about anything better. Watch how these artists use words as an embellishment to add interest and express meaning in these simply "word-y" layouts.

Father & Son Tag Booklet

BY KRISTINA

THE PROCESS:
Decorate one side of a large tag for the cover. Decorate the reverse side for the first page of the booklet. Add other decorated tags for the "pages." Clamp the tags together with small office clips.

Soar BY KRISTINA

THE PROCESS: Trim and arrange patterned papers on both sides of the layout. Overlay a transparency on the top portion of the right-hand page. Finish the layout with ribbon, a photo corner and hand-written journaling.

Love
BY JACKIE

THE PROCESS: Create a grid with cardstock strips and fill with a photo, papers and journaling. Create the journaling blocks by stamping script on kraft-colored cardstock, then printing a title on top. Decorate bookplates with buttons, linen thread and hemp cord.

2 Stories. Brick Front. 1/3 of an Acre. 4 bedrooms. 2 1/2 bathrooms. Swim & Tennis community. Nice, quiet street. Walking distance to school. Good school district. White kitchen. Keeping Room with fireplace. Hardwood floors. New condition. Wooded back yard. Horse farm behind. Nice neighbors. Huge master bedroom. My Favorite House. Studio room over the garage for me. 2-story family room

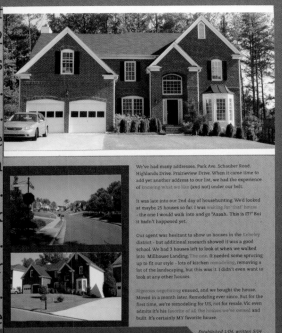

We've had many addresses. Park Ave. Schauber Road. Highlands Drive. Prairieview Drive. When it came time to add yet another address to our list, we had the experience of knowing what we like (and not) under our belt.

It was late into our 2nd day of househunting. We'd looked at maybe 25 houses so far. I was waiting for "that" house - the one I would walk into and go "Aaaah. This is IT!" But it hadn't happened yet.

Our agent was hesitant to show us houses in the Kebeley district - but additional research showed it was a good school. We had 3 houses left to look at when we walked into Millhouse Landing. The one. It needed some sprucing up to fit our style - lots of kitchen remodeling, removing a lot of the landscaping, but this was it. I didn't even want to look at any other houses.

Rigorous negotiating ensued, and we bought the house. Moved in a month later. Remodeling ever since. But for the first time, we're remodeling for US, not for resale. Vic even admits it's his favorite of all the houses we've owned and built. It's certainly MY favorite house.

Established 1/04, written 5/04

My Favorite House
BY LISA

THE PROCESS: Fill one page with text. Print on cardstock, then print the again on a transparency. Cut a rectangle in the cardstock, then adhere the transparency sheet to the back, creating a seamless stream of text. Adhere photo behind the transparency.

Refusing to Smile
BY RENEE

THE PROCESS: Block bottom of layout with patterned papers, then sew tightly around each piece. Print journaling onto cardstock and onto strips. Fold strips over the top of the cardstock base. Attach using various methods.

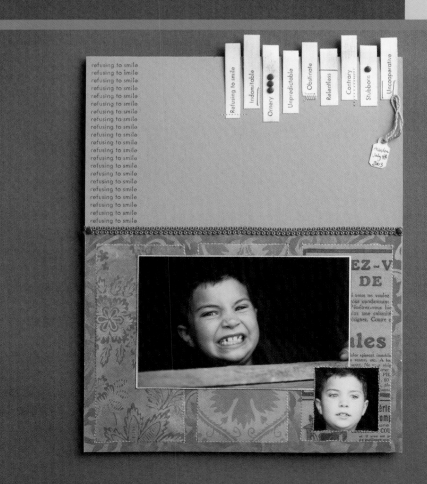

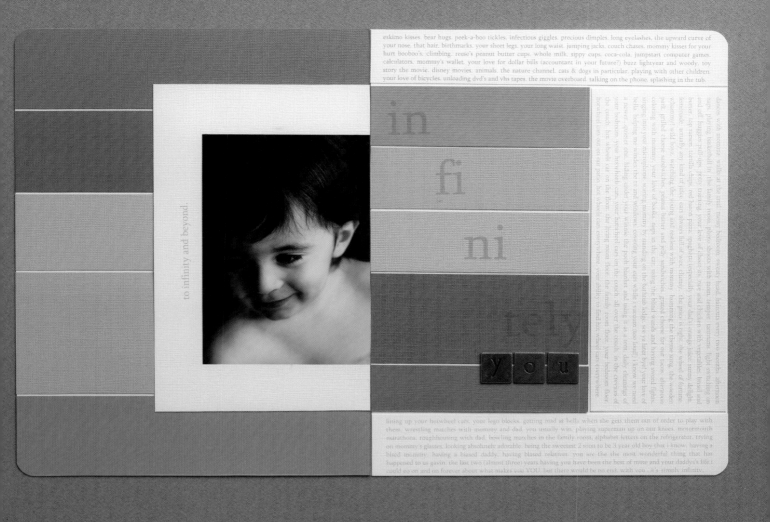

eskimo kisses. bear hugs. peek-a-boo tickles. infectious giggles. precious dimples. long eyelashes. the upward curve of your nose. that hair. birthmarks. your short legs. your long waist. jumping jacks. couch chases. mommy kisses for your hurt booboo's. climbing. reese's peanut butter cups. whole milk. sippy cups. coca-cola. jumpstart computer games. calculators. mommy's wallet. your love for dollar bills (accountant in your future?) buzz lightyear and woody. toy story the movie. disney movies. animals. the nature channel. cats & dogs in particular. playing with other children. your love of bicycles. unloading dvd's and vhs tapes. the movie overboard. talking on the phone. splashing in the tub.

to infinity and beyond.

in
fi
ni

y o u

lining up your hotswheel cars. your lego blocks. getting mad at bella when she gets them out of order to play with them. wrestling matches with mommy and dad. you usually win. playing superman up on our knees. motormouth marathons. roughhousing with dad. bowling matches in the family room. alphabet letters on the refrigerator. trying on mommy's glasses. looking absolutely adorable. being the sweetest 2 soon to be 3 year old boy that i know. having a biased mommy. having a biased daddy. having biased relatives. you are the the most wonderful thing that has happened to us gavin. the last two (almost three) years having you have been the best of mine and your daddy's life. i could go on and on forever about what makes you YOU. but there would be no end. with you. it's simply. infinity.

Infinitely You BY DESIREE

THE PROCESS: Stripe left page with cardstock, leaving a small space between each strip. Add shorter strips of cardstock to right-hand page, printing two letters from the title on each piece. Adhere journaling strips around the edges.

Miss You Lots

BY JENNIFER

THE PROCESS: Print text on patterned paper. Cut into circles and mat on cardstock, inserting ribbon between the layers. Add brads at the edges to secure.

simply words

BY JENNIFER

I enjoy creating backgrounds of words for my layouts. However, it takes quite a bit of time to collage words in different fonts. Therefore, I created a one-page document that is entirely a "word collage," and I open it whenever I need a word background. Simply create several text boxes with the words "word collage" in them. Be sure to overlap them, remove the borders and use lots of different fonts. Once you get a look you are happy with, save it. Whenever you want a background of words, open this file. Within Microsoft® Word and under Edit on the toolbar, do a "Find" for the words "word collage," and "Replace" with whatever you want your background words to be. It will instantly change them all and you will have a word collage background. Talk about simple!

Caroline
BY LISA

THE PROCESS: Create text boxes for the four words. Size and align them to fill the spaces around the photos to create one large block of photos and text.

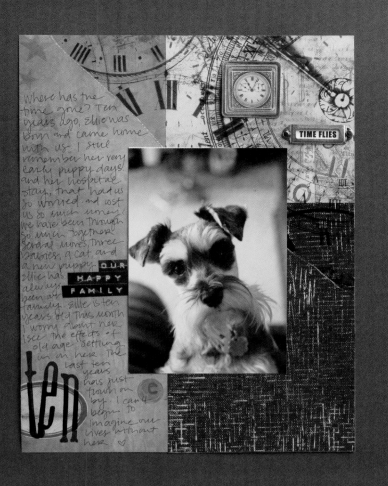

Ten

BY KRISTINA

THE PROCESS: Color block background with patterned papers. Glue photo on a printed transparency, then add over background, hiding the glue behind the photo. Rubber stamp a title over a label sticker.

Big Blue Eyes

BY RENEE

THE PROCESS: Print a title in reverse, then cut out. Attach double-sided sticky paper to the front of each letter and trim off excess. Remove protective covering, then dip into blue beads, pressing down to seal them to the adhesive. Accent rectangle word strips with ribbon.

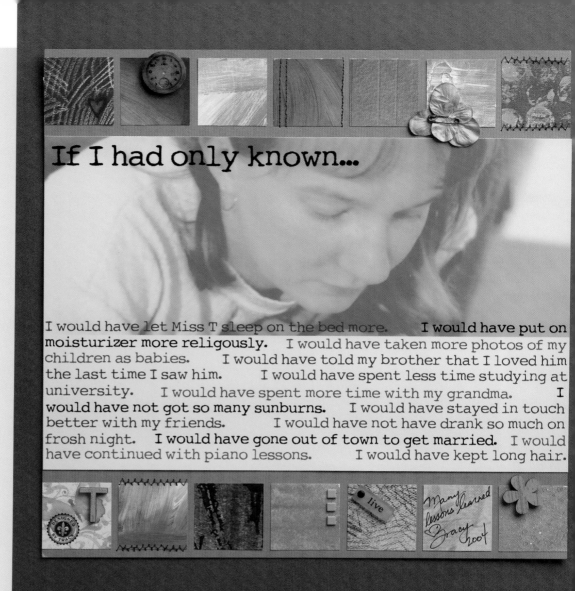

If I had only known...

I would have let Miss T sleep on the bed more.   I would have put on moisturizer more religously.   I would have taken more photos of my children as babies.   I would have told my brother that I loved him the last time I saw him.   I would have spent less time studying at university.   I would have spent more time with my grandma.   I would have not got so many sunburns.   I would have stayed in touch better with my friends.   I would have not have drank so much on frosh night.   I would have gone out of town to get married.   I would have continued with piano lessons.   I would have kept long hair.

If I Had Only Known

BY TRACY

THE PROCESS:
Desaturate a photo with photo-editing software. Add title and journaling on top and underneath the photo, then print on photo paper. Add embellished squares of patterned paper.

Kiss

BY TRACY

THE PROCESS: Stamp diamond shapes at the top with VersaMark ink, then print journaling. Print a K on cork by first adhering it to a sheet of paper. Cut out and burn the edges with a Hot Boss. Use the Hot Boss to burn letters into cork. Zigzag a cork title to layout.

Childhood BY NIA

THE PROCESS: Print journaling in black on white paper, then again in a green text box with white text. Print a quotation in white text within a teal-filled text box, cut into strips and use to separate the journaling areas. Print title, then overlay a piece of patterned vellum.

Summer Daydreams
BY NIA

THE PROCESS: Print journaling in a black font on white paper, then again on orange, burgundy and teal paper with a white font. Cut into squares, then use a circle punch to overlap areas of the journaling so it looks like one piece.

simply patterned

In the past, mixing patterns was a major fashion faux pas; the striped shirt and plaid pants were a definite no-go. Today, a patterned pairing is au courant. In fact, mixing patterns is not only fun, the results can be fabulous. Keeping the patterns in the same color or tone prevents them from overwhelming your photos. Just one look at Desiree's *So Sassy* layout, and you'll be rethinking your patterned paper stash.

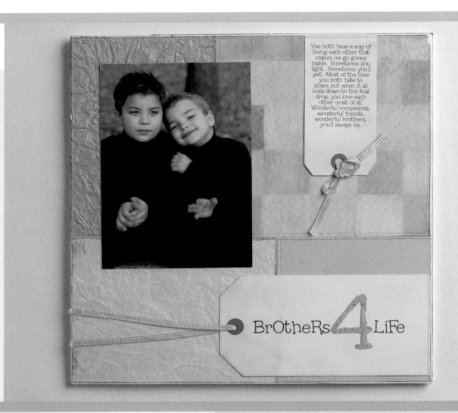

Brothers For Life
BY RENEE

THE PROCESS:
Machine stitch blocks of patterned papers to a cardstock base. Print journaling and title onto tags, leaving a space between the title for a hand-cut "4" to be inserted. Attach tags to page by sewing around the edges of the layout.

Sweet Baby Girl
BY JACKIE

THE PROCESS:
Arrange photo and patterned papers onto cardstock. Use letter stickers for "baby girl." Print "sweet" onto a transparency and lay on top to complete the title.

oh

so

sassy

yet

so

sweet

So Sassy BY DESIREE

THE PROCESS:
Layer patterned papers behind a half circle cut into white cardstock. Trim the photo to
follow the curve of the circle. Attach patterned paper above and below photo, also
following the curve. Add brads, a cut out letter and a title printed on patterned paper.

A Passion For Flowers
BY RENEE

THE PROCESS: Trim patterned paper to fit onto patterned cardstock background. Edge each piece with ink and attach to page. Machine stitch along the edges of a few blocks. Use letter stickers for the title.

Madie
BY KRISTINA

THE PROCESS: Color block background with various papers. Back a metal frame and metal-rimmed tag with patterned paper. For a fun touch, punch a square in the background and back with a coordinating patterned paper.

delaney 2004

discovering gloss

Discover Gloss
BY TRACY

THE PROCESS:
Attach strips of patterned papers to cardstock on a diagonal. Add a photo and rub-on title.

simply patterned

BY JACKIE

I'm not sure that there are actual "rules" when using patterned papers. I like to take each layout for itself and decide the feel I'd like to create. Sometimes I will look to my photos for help in choosing papers. If they are sunny, outdoor photos of the kids, I might mix something bright and orange to convey the warmth of the sun with blue patterns representing the sky, then add greens and browns to pick up the earth and foliage. If I'm doing a baby boy layout, I might mix checks with stripes and paisleys but try to have a shade of blue represented. I have created more than one layout by using up whatever bits happened to be left over on my desk. I like having unexpected paper choices in my layouts as well. Experiment a little; try to break out of your comfort zone and see what happens!

Yummy Italian
BY JENNIFER

THE PROCESS:
Cut strips of patterned paper to look like ribbon. Line up the strips, adding a few strips of real ribbon. Stamp flower images directly on the paper and ribbon.

My mom and I love to go out for an evening in downtown Cincinnati. On this gorgeous April night, we went with my dad and Ken for a huge Italian dinner at Palominos and to see Josh Groban, who sings beautiful songs in Italian. We had such fun. My mom and I are still trying to decide which we enjoyed more... the yummy Italian dinner or the yummy guy singing in Italian.
April 2004

Love
BY KRISTINA

THE PROCESS: Trim and tear patterned papers to create a heart shape. Color block the opposite page with coordinating patterned paper. Adhere ribbon and a printed transparency over the pieced heart. Embellish page with a wax seal, photo corner and heart charm.

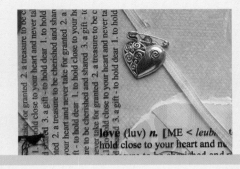

The BIG picture: This is what it all comes down to...the photo. With passion for photography reaching fever pitch, it's high time for the photos to take center stage. How better to do it than with clean-lined projects that will give them the attention they deserve? Make them huge, full-bleed or panoramic; color them, Photoshop™ them or use them to make amazing photo transfers. Just make sure the photos are the focus. Get the picture?

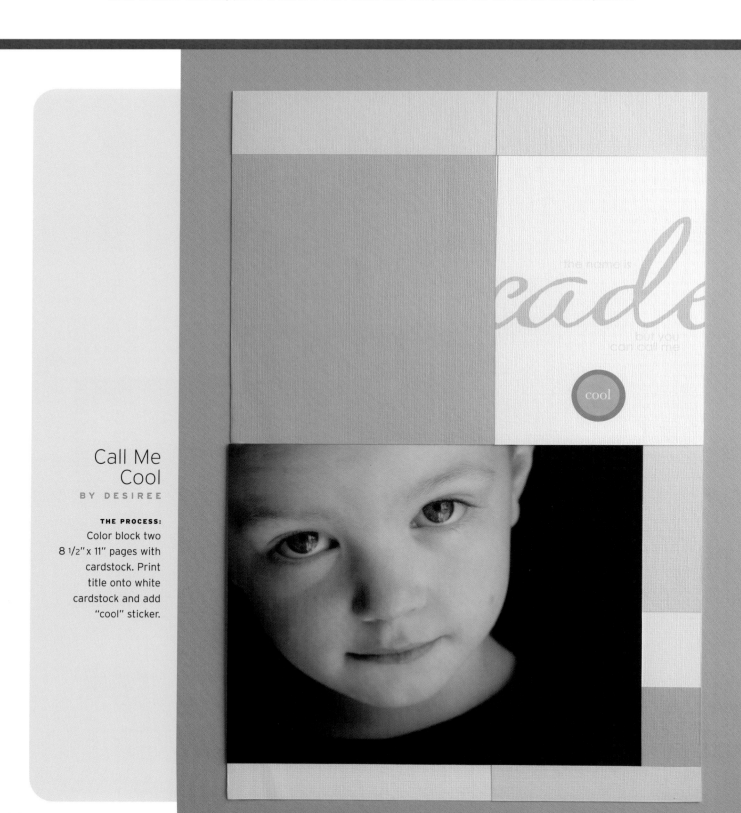

Call Me Cool
BY DESIREE

THE PROCESS: Color block two 8 1/2" x 11" pages with cardstock. Print title onto white cardstock and add "cool" sticker.

Thirty One BY KRISTINA

THE PROCESS: Enlarge a photo to page size. Trim a transparency to 8 1/2" x 11". Adhere photo strip to the transparency, then adhere to the background paper, hiding the glue behind the photo strip. Attach vellum over the top and use letter stickers for the title.

Panoramic Photo Cards
BY LISA

THE PROCESS: Resize and crop photos to a small panorama size (2 1/2" x 5 1/2".) Using a graphics or word-processing program, type text to fill the space above and below the photo, creating a square. Adhere photo to the middle.

Just Me
BY TRACY

THE PROCESS:
Cut a transparency into strips and paint the back very roughly with different colors. Print journaling on a few strips and add rub-ons to the rest. In a photo-editing program, add title to photo and print as 8" x 12".

Pears
BY JENNIFER B.

THE PROCESS:
Scan pear image and apply an artistic edge. Resize and print onto a transparency. Apply paint to metal flashing. Let dry. Attach transparency to metal with eyelets. Connect three sections with bead chain and add a chain hanger to the top piece.

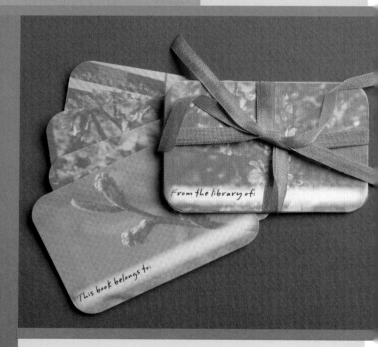

Gift Bookplates
BY LISA

THE PROCESS: Scan or open digital images in a photo-editing program. Resize to 3 1/2" x 2", and set transparency to 60%. Add a text box with white fill, black text and a feathered border.

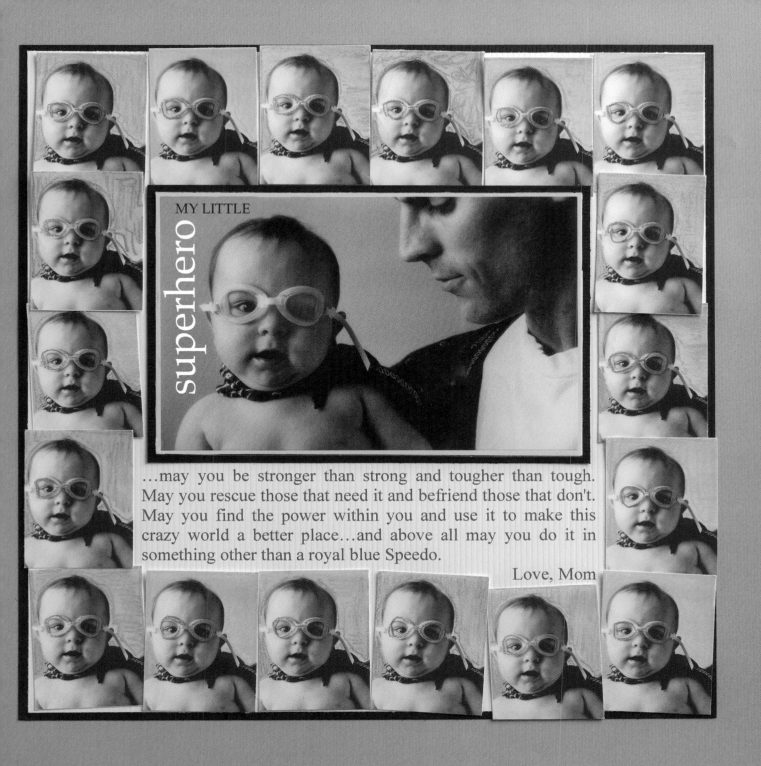

MY LITTLE
superhero

...may you be stronger than strong and tougher than tough. May you rescue those that need it and befriend those that don't. May you find the power within you and use it to make this crazy world a better place...and above all may you do it in something other than a royal blue Speedo.

Love, Mom

My Little Superhero
BY RUTH

THE PROCESS: Print photos on watercolor paper. Color with watercolor crayons and wet with a paintbrush.

The Look
BY RUTH

THE PROCESS:
Add a border to a photo using photo-editing software. Punch holes in linen paper, thread with wire and use to mat the journaling.

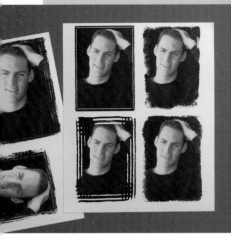

It's the "how could you be so silly-ridiculous-funny-loveable-sexy-outrageous-wonderful and oh so you?" look that I love. It's the happy moment, the riotous laughter, and the "everything will be o.k." look. I love that look. I love you Eric.

THE LOOK

simply shot
BY KRISTINA

My favorite kind of photograph is the shot that is completely candid – not posed in any way. It is during these candid moments that I capture the most intense expressions, emotions and displays of personality. I love to catch the everyday things in the life around me: the way my kids really look on Saturdays, the craziness of my weekday mornings and the messy smiles while eating our large Sunday breakfast. I have not always understood photography and all of the mechanics of the art, but I recently had the opportunity to watch a talented photographer, Tara Whitney, take a whole day's worth of candid shots. I learned so much watching her use the natural light and background of my home to capture wonderful photos. Most importantly, I learned that although a photo is taken candidly, it can still be a work of art – a simple statement about everyday life.

The Stuff of Life BY TRACY

THE PROCESS: With photo-editing software, crop and merge photos to create a 12″ x 12″ image. Split the image into two, and have developed at a lab. Cut photos apart and arrange on page. Attach transparency on top and add title with rub-ons.

Scrapping Must Haves

BY DESIREE

THE PROCESS:
In a photo-editing program, create a custom negative strip and print onto photo paper. Roll up and place in film canister. Add a custom label to an envelope. Tie mini photos with ribbon and place inside envelope.

Just a Little Somethin'

BY NIA

THE PROCESS: Create a mini pocket from a slide frame protector sheet. Tuck index print strips in the pocket. Using a template, create the envelope, using a mini photo on the tag.

Almost 4
BY JENNIFER B.

THE PROCESS:
Create background from patterned papers. Put brads in backwards for embellishment. Add photo and negative strip over an envelope. Back a stencil with patterned paper. Rubber stamp on twill and place under stencil.

Welcome Roxie
BY JENNIFER

THE PROCESS: In photo-editing software, reduce photos to the same size and arrange in rows. Add text down one row. Make paw print on envelope using circle stamps.

artist bios simplified

Lisa Russo

Originally from upstate New York, Lisa currently makes her home in Marietta, Georgia, with her son Aidan and husband of ten years, Victor. A 2003 inductee into the *Creating Keepsakes* Hall of Fame, Lisa is also a Garden Girl at Two Peas in a Bucket and a contributing artist for the DW books. In her spare time, Lisa delights in reading, gardening and organizing.

TIP: Invest in disposable cleaning wipes. I keep them in every room of my house, and when something looks a little dirty, I wipe and toss.

TIP: I am "simple" challenged; my motto is "anything worth doing is worth overdoing." I do try to simplify, however, by using what I already have because you don't have to spend time and money at the store and it forces you to be creative.

Debbie Crouse

Debbie lives in Gilbert, Arizona, with her husband Skip. She is the proud mother of Logan, Skyler, Emali and Jared, favorite mother-in-law to Kathy and spoiling grandma to Cole, Will and Carter. Debbie has been an artist for the "Designing With" series from its genesis.

Jennifer McGuire

Jennifer lives in Cincinnati, Ohio, where she works as a full-time scrapbooker and stamper for Autumn Leaves and Hero Arts. A 2002 *Creating Keepsakes* Hall of Fame inductee, Jennifer loves traveling around the world teaching classes, and she can often be found at Two Peas in a Bucket, where she designs projects and fonts. Jennifer is the proud "step-mum" of Kay and Audrey, blessed wife of Ken and friend of Roxie, her new Vizsla puppy.

TIP: I find my life was best simplified by marrying Ken; he does the laundry, ironing and picking-up!

TIP: One of my best tips for simplifying life is getting rid of the clutter. If you get rid of things you don't just love anymore or that take up unnecessary space, you'll have an easier time cleaning up when you finally DO have time to clean.

Renee Camacho

Renee resides in Nashville with her amazingly supportive husband, gorgeous children and hopefully gorgeous-by-summer flower beds. A 2002 *Creating Keepsakes* Hall of Fame inductee, Renee designs products for Autumn Leaves and is a contributing artist for the DW books. In her spare time, she photographs others, gardens, helps with her church activities and sings.

Kristina Nicolai-White

Kristina calls Madison, Wisconsin her home where she lives with her husband, Jeffrey, their three kids and two dogs. Kristina is the owner of Two Peas in a Bucket, an online scrapbooking community. When not working, she keeps herself busy reading and spending time with her family.

TIP: Keep a very detailed calendar. Keeping accurate track of all the appointments, meetings, school functions, as well as meal plans saves so much time.

TIP: My life is most simple when I follow the mantra "carry less baggage"—meaning collect fewer things in my home, purse, car and life. It allows me to pay attention to the things and people that matter most.

Ruth Giauque

A resident of Gilbert, Arizona, Ruth is married to a wonderful man, Eric, and is the mom to four energetic and darling children, Hana, Mikenna, Christian and Noah. Ruth's interests include playing with her kids, photography, paper arts, teaching workshops at Memory Lane, playing the violin and getting to know all the fabulous people along the way.

Tracy Kyle

Tracy lives in Mission, British Columbia, with her husband, Dan, and two children, Tristan and Isabella. A civil engineer, *Creating Keepsakes* 2003 Hall of Fame inductee, *Better Homes and Gardens* team member and Garden Girl at Two Peas in a Bucket, Tracy savors taking photos, spending time outside and staying up late watching movies.

TIP: Give every item in your house a "home," so everyone knows where to put it.

Cathy Blackstone

Cathy is a stay-at-home mom in Columbus, Ohio, to Jackson, Ellie and Brynn. Soon after Jackson was born, she thought she would make a little scrapbook about his first year. Ha! What once was a hobby is now a full-blown obsession – an obsession that has granted her amazing opportunities and friendships. Some of her closest friendships have been made as a result of being a Garden Girl for Two Peas in a Bucket.

TIP: Pick and choose your battles. I do it all day long and it makes my life a bit easier.

TIP: Whether leaving for a day trip or just getting the kids out the door for school, get as much as possible ready the night before–clothes laid out, lunches started, backpacks ready by the door. It gets mornings off on a much nicer pace when things are preplanned.

Jackie Bonette

Jackie lives in Taber, Alberta, Canada, with Bernie, her husband of nine years, and their three very active children, Ren, Kallee and Cole. Jackie is also a Garden Girl at Two Peas in a Bucket. Reading, shopping and, of course, scrapbooking fill any extra time she finds.

Jennifer Bester

Jennifer has been scrapbooking for almost four years, having started right after the birth of her first child. After winning *Creating Keepsakes* Hall of Fame in 2003, Jennifer has stayed busy working on her albums. She, her husband, Dave, and daughter, Franny, live in Reading, Massachusetts, and are eagerly awaiting the newest member of their family due to arrive in July.

TIP: The way I simplify my life is by having a clean, mini-malist approach to furnishing and decorating my home. The fewer things I have out, the less there is to dust.

TIP: The perfect tool for simplifying my life is the book *365 Ways to Relax Mind, Body and Soul*. It gives ideas for each day of the year to help calm and relax your mind, body and spirit.

Desiree McClellan

Originally from Missouri, Desiree currently resides in Decatur, Alabama, with her son, Gavin, and husband of four years, James. During her scrapbooking career of two years, Desiree's work has been seen in *Creating Keepsakes, Simple Scrapbooks, Scrapbooks Etc., Ivy Cottage* and *Memory Makers*. In her free time, Desiree can be found taking photos, reading or playing the piano.

Stacy McFadden

Stacy McFadden is an American living in Melbourne, Australia, with her husband, Tom, and three sons, Nicholas, Zachary and Joshua. Stacy has been scrapbooking for seven years and was delighted to receive an honorable mention in the *Creating Keepsakes* 2004 Hall Of Fame. She and her family are enjoying living "down under," and they love traveling around the country to experience its beauty and diversity.

TIP: To live simply, I have a periodic "cleaning out" to get rid of unused items. Whether it's scrapbook supplies or household clutter, I always feel so much better after I have sorted and purged.

TIP: My best tip for simplifying life is post-it notes. I am an avid post-it note user. I write reminder notes to myself and keep them on the fridge, so I always remember the things on my to-do list.

Nia Reddy

Nia lives in Brooklyn, New York, with her two year-old "little man," Aiden, and her tech-savvy and adorably cute husband, Alvaro. Nia began scrapbooking in the fall of 2002 and is honored to be an inductee into the 2004 *Creating Keepsakes* Hall of Fame. Nia has an affinity for shopping, photography and collecting ribbon.

Julie van Oosten

Julie lives in Perth, Western Australia, with her husband, Rob, and their sixteen year-old twin girls, Danielle and Lauren. With a love for paper, miniatures and rubber stamps, Julie has designed a range of products and has been published in *Somerset Studio, Artistry with Rubber Stamps* and *The Rubber Gazette*. Julie's passions include jewelry, artistamps, miniature books and designing.

TIP: I am fortunate to travel a lot, so I have a small plastic bag filled with all of my toiletries, adaptors, etc. (in miniature, of course!). All I need to remember when packing is to throw that little bag in my suitcase.

product credits

1

simply sophisticated
Pages 4-7

SOUL DEEP
STICKERS: CI and MAMBI
PAPER: 7gypsies
RUBBER STAMP: Savvy Stamps
PHOTO CORNER: MM
PHOTOS: Daniela Berkhout

RYAN
PHOTOS: Daniela Berkhout

PASTA GIFT SET
FONTS: Goudy Old Style and Hootie

SOME LIKE IT HOT
FONTS: Dirty Ego and Impact

GOOFBALL AHEAD
FONT: Impact
PAPER: Inspire2 and KI Memories
STICKERS: Inspire2

FAMILY
FONTS: Garamond, Edwardian Script
PAPER: MAMBI
FRAME: Nunn Designs
RIBBON: Kate's Paperie
PHOTOS: Denitra Moore

HUSBAND AND WIFE
WOOD LETTER: Walnut Hollow
TRANSPARENCY & ACRYLIC WORDS: CI
EMBOSSED VELLUM: K & Co.

2

simply hip
Pages 8-13

FLOWER CHILD SAVANNAH
PAPER: KI Memories
BUTTONS: Junkitz
PHOTOS: Tara Pakosta

DON'T LET WEEDS GROW
FONTS: Landscape, Songwriter and Uncle Charles, AL

ALWAYS KEILAH
PHOTOS: Nely Fok
PAPER: KI Memories
METAL FLOWER AND BEAD CHAIN: MM
RUBBER STAMP: Postmodern Design
WOVEN LABEL: MAMBI
FLOWER PHOTO: A Slice of Pie

SPIRIT
VELLUM: American Crafts
FONTS: Fontdinerdotcom Sparkly and Helvetica

SPLASH
PAPER: Doodlebug and KI Memories
FONT: Fontdinerdotcom Sparkly

MODERN MAN
FONT: Trajan Pro, Photoshop

SPEEDY LITTLE AUDREY
FONT: Uncle Charles, AL
RUBBER STAMPS: The Blue Hand

JOURNAL
EMBOSSING TEMPLATES: Lasting Impression
WOOD LETTER: Walnut Hollow

WHEN DID I GROW UP?
PHOTO: Tara Whitney
FONTS: Landscape, AL; 2Peas Yo-Yo
WOOD FLOWERS: Li'l Davis Designs

STITCHED CARD SET
FONT: Helvetica Neue

FRIENDS
FONT: Perspective Sans

3

simply soft
Pages 14-19

TICKLED PINK
RIBBON AND TAG: 7gypsies
RUBBER STAMPS: Impress Rubber Stamps
CLEAR BOX: Impact Images

6
PAPER AND VELLUM: AL
RUBBER STAMP: Postmodern Design
RIBBON AND PHOTO TURNS: 7gypsies
BUBBLE LETTER: Li'l Davis Designs

LILLI
FONTS: P22 Typewriter, P22 Type Foundry; Elegant
PAPER: AL
RIBBON: 7gypsies

JUST A LITTLE GUIDANCE
FONT: P22 Typewriter, P22 Type Foundry
PAPER: Paper Loft, Paper Adventures and 7gypsies
RUBBER STAMPS: Just for Fun, MM, River City Rubber Works and Stamps Happen
PHOTO TURN: 7gypsies

AGE 8
RUBBER STAMPS: Hero Arts
PAPER FLOWERS: Savvy Stamps
ENAMELED NUMBER: Ballard Designs
PAPER: AL and Jennifer Collection

ALMOST 2
PATTERNED PAPER: AL
METAL TIN: Artistic Expressions
RIBBON: Kate's Paperie
FONTS: Baramond and Dirty Ego

PRINCESS
FONT: Old Remington, AL
PAPER: Anna Griffin and 7gypsies
TITLE LETTERS: Mustard Moon

BABY GABRIELLE
PAPER: AL and 7gypsies
BOOK PLATE, RIBBON AND NAIL HEAD: 7gypsies

FAMILY FARM
PAPER: 7gypsies and The Paper Loft
TAG: 7gypsies
ALPHABET CHARM, BOOK PLATE, STICK PIN, SHAPED CLIP AND SAFETY PIN: MM
STICKERS: Chatterbox and CI
RUBBER STAMPS: Missing Link Stamp Co. and PSX Design

4

simply antique
Pages 20-23

WORDS JOURNAL
WORDS: Collections
DIMENSIONAL MAGIC: Plaid

LORENE ADELLE
FONT: 2Peas Katherine Ann
BUTTONS: Nostalgiques
PAPER: AL
RIBBON: MM

KEETCH SISTERS
PAPER: MAMBI
PHOTO CORNERS: 7gypsies
MODELING PASTE: Liquitex
T-SHIRT TRANSFER PAPER: Epson

JACK
PAPER: MAMBI and Scrappy Chic
BOOKPLATE: Embellish It!
FONTS: P22 Cezanne, P22 Type Foundry; Dactylographe

TINY FRAME BOOK
MINI FRAME, EMBELLISHMENTS AND VINTAGE PICTURES: Collections

SWEET NOTES
PAPER: 7gypsies
RIBBON: May Arts
HEAT TOOL: Walnut Hollow
PETITE TABS, BARBED ELASTIC AND MINI TAG: 7gypsies

FRIEDA AND THE BUNNIES
FONT: Antique Type and Texas Hero
PAPER: AL and K & Co.
PRINTED TRANSPARENCY: CI
RUBBER STAMPS: River City Rubber Works

CHERISH
PAPER: K & Co.
RUBBER STAMPS: Hero Arts and Rubber Moon
FONT: Constitution, AL
CHARM: Hap's Memories

COWBOYS
LEATHER PAPER: K & Co.
PAGE CLIP: Sweetwater
PHOTO FLIPS: MM
FONTS: Gettysburg and Remington, AL

5

simply collage
Pages 24-25

TRUE FRIEND
FONT: Messenger, AL
KITTEN CLIP: ScrapYard
KITTY PAPERCLIP: Karen Foster Design
PAPER: Chatterbox
TAGS: Pebbles Inc.
CHARM: Doodlebug
RIBBON AND METAL FRAMES: MM

MISCHIEVOUS
PAPER: 7gypsies and Anna Griffin
STENCILS AND RUB-ONS: AL
RUBBER STAMPS: Hero Arts and Magenta

ME & MY GIRLS
RIBBON: Scrapbook Wizard
PAPER & FRENCH ENAMEL: 7gypsies
RUBBER STAMPS: PSX Design
METAL FRAME: CI

REMEMBER WHEN CARD
PAPER: 7gypsies
RIBBON: May Arts and Mokuba
HEMP AND WAXED LINEN: 7gypsies
FONT: 2Peas David Walker

6
simply secrets
Pages 26-29

CHOCOLATE BOOK
SILVER HANDLE, HEART SPIRALS, RIBBON, WAXED LINEN AND PAPER: 7gypsies
ENVELOPES: Waste Not Paper
RUBBER STAMPS: MaVinci's Reliquary
ENVELOPES: Envelopments

ALMOST TWO
PAPER: Paper Loft, K & Co., Rusty Pickle, 7gypsies and Sweetwater
STICKERS: Sticker Studio and 7gypsies
SYNONYM TABS: AL

A @ K
PAPER: AL, Paper Fever, CI and KI Memories
STICKERS: CI, MM, KI Memories, American Craft, Scrapbook Wizard and Wordsworth
RUBBER STAMPS: PSX Design
FLOWER AND HINGES: MM
RUB-ONS: AL

GROOVY LOVE
FONTS: Inspiration and Dustismo
PHOTO: Jessi Stringham

AFTERNOON AT THE LAKE
FONT: 2Peas Renaissance
STICKERS: MAMBI
PAPER: Scrapbook Wizard
METAL CORNERS: MM

MOM'S FLOWERS
PAPER: Paper Loft
ALTERED BOOK TILES: Collections
ENCLOSURE LABEL & LEDGER PAPER: Manto Fev
RUB-ONS: AL

7
simply clear
Pages 30-35

SUN
STICKERS: CI
WOOD PAPER: Lenderink Industries

FLOWERS
PAPER: K & Co.
TRANSPARENCY: CI
ENVELOPE: Soho Paper Company
RUBBER STAMPS: PSX Design
METAL END CLAMP: 7gypsies

SING
FONT: Trajan Pro, Photoshop

HEARTBEAT
FONTS: Pooh and Clarissa
TRANSPARENCY: Artistic Expressions
RUBBER STAMPS: Hero Arts and JudiKins

TRANSPARENCY BOOKLET
RUB-ON WORDS: What's New
LIBRARY POCKETS: Li'l Davis Designs
PAPER: CI, Anna Griffin, 7gypsies and Karen Foster Design
CIRCLE: Junkitz

CARDS
TRANSPARENCY: Daisy D's
RIBBON: May Arts
CHARM: Quest Beads and MM
STICKER: Pebbles Inc.

FACES OF YOU
FONT: Francine HMK Bold

IN YOUR EYES
FONT: Inkburrow
PAPER AND VELLUM: AL
WATCH FACE: 7gypsies

NICHOLAS
TRANSPARENCY: Artistic Expressions
FONTS: 1942 Report, Dirty Ego, Texas Hero, American Typewriter and Papyrus; P22 Cezanne, P22 Type Foundry

LOT #291
RIBBON AND TAG: 7gypsies

8
simply silly
Pages 36-39

DADDY...MOMMY HAS A BABY
FONT: Old Remington, AL
CHARMS: Quest Beads

BOP-IT
PHOTOS: Nely Fok
FONT: 2Peas Tasklist and 2Peas Variety Show
CONCHOS: 7gypsies

LITTLE BEHIND
PAPER: SEI
RIBBON: Makuba

TRUE STORY DVD CASE
PAPER: Cross My Heart and MOD
TAG: Paperbilities
TRANSPARENCY & WORDS STICKER: CI
FONT: 2Peas Tasklist

LITTLEST BOTTOM
PAPER: Chatterbox and Anna Griffin
RUBBER STAMPS: Hero Arts
BUTTONS: Junkitz
PINS, WOOD FLOWER AND LETTER: Li'l Davis Designs
PAPER FLOWERS: Savvy Stamps
FONT: Updated Classic, AL
PHOTO: Angela Talentino

NEW ZEALAND TRAFFIC JAM
FONT: Apple Chancery
STICKERS: MAMBI and Scrappy Chic

HAIR SALAD
FONTS: Fontesque and Disturbance

9
simply colorful
Pages 40-43

MORE THAN I EVER IMAGINED
FONT: 2peas Rickety
STICKERS: K & Co. and Doodlebug Designs

GIFT TAG AND BOX SET
TILES, MINI FRAMES AND TYPEWRITER CIRCLES: Collections

BRYNN
PIN: MM
FONT: Bookman Headline BT

HARMONY
PAPER: CI, Anna Griffin, KI Memories and K & Co.
TRANSPARENCY: Magic Scraps
STAMPS: Missing Link Stamp Co.
STICKER: CI
METAL CLAMP AND PHOTO TURNS: 7gypsies

J & C
FONTS: Highlight, AL; 2Peas Fancy Free
HANDMADE PAPER: Artistic Scrapper
CONCHO AND WORD: Scrapworks

VIVID COLOR
FONT: Rockwell

THE BLUZ
WATERCOLOR PAPER: Strathmore
FONT: John Doe
WATERCOLORS: Dr. Ph. Martin's

10
simply stitched
Pages 44-47

FLEUR CARD
RUBBER STAMPS: Paper Impressions and Wordsworth
NOTE CARD & ENVELOPE: Hero Arts

CHEEKWOOD ARCHITECTURE
BUTTONS: 7gypsies
PAPER: AL and Pebbles Inc.
WAXY THREAD: 7gypsies
FONT: Messenger, AL

CHANNING
PAPER: AL and Jennifer Collection
FONT: Post Master, AL

LOVES ME, LOVES ME NOT
WATERCOLOR PAPER: Strathmore
RIBBON: 7gypsies

MACKENZIE
PHOTOS: Daniela Berkhout
FONT: 2Peas Flea Market
STICKERS: CI, MAMBI, Doodlebug
Designs and Nostalgiques
PAPER: Paper Fever, KI Memories and
7gypsies
METAL LETTER AND BUTTON: MM
TYPEWRITER KEY: CI

HUGGING
FONT: 2Peas Ragtag
RUBBER STAMP: Savvy Stamps

ONE YEAR OLD
WOOD FLOWERS: Li'l Davis Designs
FONT: 2Peas Flea Market
FLOWER BRADS: MM
LETTERS: FoofaLa
RIBBON: 7gypsies
TAGS: Pebbles Inc.

LOVEABLE
TRANSPARENCY: CI
VELLUM: AL
ACRYLIC HEART: KI Memories

11

simply stamped
Pages 48-51

CHERISH THE MOMENT
RUBBER STAMPS: Limited Edition
Rubber Stamps and Magenta
RUB-ONS: Déjà Views
PHOTO TURN: 7gypsies
TIE UPS: EK Success
WOVEN CORNER: MM
PAPER: Anna Griffin, 7gypsies,
Magenta, EK Success and
Scrappin' Dreams
PHOTOS: Irma Gabbard

CREATE
STAMPS: Making Tracks, Postmodern
Design, Hero Arts, Stampin' Up!,
Hampton Art Stamps, Stamp Craft,
Wisecracks and Stampers
Anonymous
PAPER AND TABS: 7gypsies
FONT: 2Peas Renaissance

FRANNY'S PLAYHOUSE
TEXTURED BRAYER: Fiskars
FONTS: 2Peas Harlequin, 2Peas Mister
Giggles and 2Peas Flea Market
HOUSE ACCENTS: Meri Meri

GIGGLE
GIGGLE TAB: AL
PAPER: KI Memories
POCKET ENVELOPE: Nostalgiques
"A" STAMP: Limited Edition Rubber
Stamps
FACE STAMP: Hampton Arts
RIBBON: Offray
FONT: Baramond

REMARKABLE
RUBBER STAMPS: Hero Arts
and JudiKins
POWDERED PIGMENT: Pearl-Ex,
Jacquard Products
PHOTO TURNS: 7gypsies
DEFINITION: MM
PHOTO: Angela Talentino

ROSES
FONT: P22 Typewriter,
P22 Type Foundry
PAPER: K & Co.
RUBBER STAMPS: River City Rubber
Works and Postmodern Design

J & C
PAPER: 7gypsies and Paper Loft
RUBBER STAMPS: MM, PSX Design,
Hero Arts and Stampers Anonymous
GOLD FRAME: 7gypsies
HINGES: MM

BOOTS
RUBBER STAMPS: Ma Vinci's
Reliquary, All Night Media and PSX
Design

12

simply petite
Pages 52-59

A PERFECT TRIP
FONTS: Love Letter TW and
Smargana Dealing
BUSINESS CARD POCKETS:
Wilson Jones
RIBBON: So Good

PARK PLAY
PAPER AND LETTER STICKER:
American Crafts
BEAD CHAIN & METAL-RIMMED TAG: MM
WOODEN FLOWER: Li'l Davis Designs

MANILLA TAG BOOK
PAPER AND PETITE FRAMES:
KI Memories

FAMILY TIN
STICKER: Pebbles Inc.
FONT: 2Peas Renaissance

FILE DIVIDER BOOK
MINI FILE DIVIDER, EMBELLISHMENTS,
RUBBER STAMP & TILES: Collections

THE SCHOOL YEARS
FONT: 2Peas Fat Frog and 2Peas Class Act
TWILL: Creekbank Creations

POCKETBOOK
FONT: Dirty Ego

HAPPY THOUGHTS
ACCORDION ALBUM: Kolo
CLEAR BUTTONS AND WAXED LINEN:
7gypsies
TAG PUNCH: CI
NUMBERS: Li'l Davis Designs
RUBBER STAMPS: Renaissance Art
Stamps, PSX Design, All Night Media
and Ma Vinci's Reliquary

COMPENDIUM BOOK
VELLUM: AL
EMBELLISHMENTS AND TAGS:
Collections

LIFETIME
PHOTO: Sharon Soneff
PAPER: CI and 7gypsies
ALPHABET STAMPS: Ma Vinci's
Reliquary, PSX Design and MM
STICKERS: Pebbles Inc., 7gypsies
and Sticker Studio
INDEX TAB, METAL END CLAMP AND
TISSUE: 7gypsies

FOB WATCH
EMBELLISHMENTS AND RUBBER
STAMP: Collections

13

simply tied
Pages 60-67

JUST BE
RIBBON: Offray
RUB-ON: Chatterbox
PAPER: AL
METAL RIMMED TAG: MM
STICKER: Pebbles Inc.

GREEN
PAPER: KI Memories
RIBBON: Impress Rubber Stamps
and MM
FONT: American Typewriter

TRUE STYLE
TRANSPARENCY: Magic Scraps
RIBBON: Offray
METAL RIMMED TAG: Avery
FONTS: Bomboni and Futura

GIFT
FONT: 2peas Sweet Pea
RUBBER STAMP: EK Success
DATE STAMP, SILK FLOWERS AND
PINS: MM
RIBBON: May Arts and 7gypsies

**CAREFREE
COMPANIONS**
RUBBER STAMP: JudiKins
RUB-ONS: MM
FLOWER: KI Memories

ASPEN TRAVEL FOLIO
FONT: P22 Typewriter, P22 Type
Foundry
PAPER: Anna Griffin

TRAVEL
PAPER: AL
PHOTO TURN AND PRINTED TWILL:
7gypsies
STICKERS: MAMBI
DEFINITION, RIBBON AND ALPHABET
CHARM: MM

MY DOG
METAL MESH: Paragona
BOOK PLATES: Li'l Davis Designs
FONT: Facelift

CHRISTIAN
PAPER: KI Memories and 7gypsies
MINI FRAME: 7gypsies
RUBBER STAMPS: PSX Design

Products without a credit are either part of the artist's personal stash or not available for purchase.

NOTE: All walnut ink is from 7gypsies. And unless otherwise noted, all computer fonts are downloaded from the Internet. 2Peas fonts are downloaded from www.twopeasinabucket.com and CK fonts are from *Creating Keepsakes*.

LEGEND
AL= Autumn Leaves
CI= Creative Imaginations
MAMBI= me and my BIG ideas
MM= Making Memories

HAPPILY EVER AFTER
PAPER: KI Memories
RUBBER STAMPS: PSX Design
BARBED ELASTICS: 7gypsies

DANKE SCHOEN
CONCHOS: 7gypsies
STICKER: Wordsworth

simply words
Pages 68-75

FATHER & SON TAG BOOKLET
PAPER: Daisy D's, Anna Griffin, SEI and Rusty Pickle
TRANSPARENCY: Magic Scraps
STICKERS: Pebbles Inc., Sticker Studio, Chatterbox, MM and Doodlebug Designs
METAL FRAME: Scrapworks
METAL CLAMP AND PHOTO TURN: 7gypsies
PHOTOS: Tara Whitney

SOAR
PAPER: AL and Carolee's Creations
FONT: 2Peas Weathervane

LOVE
PAPER: AL and Li'l Davis Designs
RUBBER STAMP: Inkadinkado
BOOKPLATES: Two Peas in a Bucket
BUTTONS: MM
LINEN THREAD: Hillcreek Designs
FONTS: 2Peas Weathervane, 2Peas My Muse, 2Peas Tasklist, 2Peas Flea Market and Typewriter

MY FAVORITE HOUSE
FONT: Caecilia

REFUSING TO SMILE
PAPER: CI and 7gypsies

INFINITELY YOU
FONT: Sylfaen
PEWTER LETTERS: MM

MISS YOU LOTS
FONTS: 2Peas Mister Giggles and 2Peas Fancy Free
PAPER: Scrapbook Wizard

CAROLINE
FONTS: P22 Typewriter, P22 Type Foundry; Problem Secretary, Hootie and American Typewriter

TEN
PAPER: AL, 7gypsies and Sweetwater
TRANSPARENCY: K & Co.
ALPHABET STAMPS: PSX Design & MM
STICKERS: Pebbles Inc. and 7gypsies
TAG AND BOOK PLATE: MM
DIE CUT: DMD

BIG BLUE EYES
FONTS: 2Peas Tiny Tadpole and 2Peas Wavy Gravy
PAPER: AL and 7gypsies
STICKY PAPER: Magic Scraps

IF I HAD ONLY KNOWN
PAPER: Wordsworth, EK Success and AL
WATCH FACE, WOODEN FLOWER AND WOODEN LETTER: Li'l Davis Designs
FLOWER: MM
STUDS: Scrapworks
ACRYLIC WORD: Doodlebug Designs
RUBBER STAMP: Paper Angel
FONT: Post Master, AL

KISS
FONTS: Punch Label, Fulton Artistamp Trial, Rough Draft, Stencil, 2Peas Typo, 2Peas Chatter, 2Peas Champagne and Cheapskatefill
PAPER: CI
VELLUM: Chatterbox
PHOTO TURNS: 7gypsies
RUBBER STAMP: Magenta
HEAT TOOL: Hot Boss, Carolee's Creations
PHOTOS: Jill Beamer

CHILDHOOD
PAPER: Paper Icon
VELLUM: NRN Designs
PAPER CHARM: MM
FONT: Splendid 66
RIBBON: Paper Access

SUMMER DAYDREAMS
PHOTOS: Karon Henderson
MINI PAPER FLOWERS: Jolee's Boutique
STICKERS: Stickopotamus
FONT: Futura

simply patterned
Pages 76-81

BROTHERS FOR LIFE
FONT: 2Peas RIckety
PAPER: AL and Jennifer Collection
RIBBON: Memory Lane

SWEET BABY GIRL
PAPER: Pebbles Inc., Anna Griffin and MM
TAG: CI
STICKERS: MAMBI and CI
FONT: Stamp Act

SO SASSY
FONTS: Lucida Console and Love
PAPER: K & Co.
PHOTOS: Michele Woods

A PASSION FOR FLOWERS
PAPER: AL, NRN Designs, CI and Wordsworth
STICKERS: AL, Li'l Davis Designs & CI
RUB-ONS: CI

MADIE
PAPER: CI, Mustard Moon, Scrappin' Dreams, Daisy D's, MM, AL and Doodlebug Designs
PHOTO TURNS: 7gypsies
STICKERS: Bo Bunny Press, CI, Mrs. Grossman's and Chatterbox
DEFINITION, CHARM AND HINGES: MM
ALPHABET STAMPS: PSX Design and Ma Vinci's Reliquary
FRAME: KI Memories

DISCOVER GLOSS
RUB-ONS: Chartpak
PAPER: CI, Doodlebug, SEI, K & Co., Paper Fever, Anna Griffin, Wordsworth, AL, KI Memories, Karen Foster Design and Magenta

YUMMY ITALIAN
PAPER: Anna Griffin, CI and Daisy D's
RUBBER STAMPS: Hero Arts
FONT: Uncle Charles, AL

LOVE
PAPER: AL, Mustard Moon, K & Co., CI, Chatterbox and Anna Griffin
TRANSPARENCY: Daisy D's
WAX SEAL: CI
CHARM: Embellish It!
ALPHABET STAMPS: PSX Design

simply shot
Pages 82-89

CALL ME COOL
FONT: Heber, Chatterbox
STICKER: American Crafts
PHOTO: Michele Woods

THIRTY ONE
PAPER: 7gypsies
TRANSPARENCY: CI
STICKERS: Wordsworth
VELLUM: AL
PHOTOS: Tara Whitney

JUST ME
RUB-ON LETTERS: MM
PAPER FLOWERS: Saavy Stamps
FONTS: Oxygen, Sandra and Young Crafter, AL; 2Peas Proud Papa
PHOTO: Tristan Bucchiotti

PEARS
BEAD CHAIN: Coffee Break Designs
COMPUTER SOFTWARE: Auto F/X Edges

GIFT BOOKPLATES
FONT: DesertDogHmk
RIBBON: 7gypsies

MY LITTLE SUPERHERO
WATERCOLOR CRAYONS: Staedtler

THE LOOK
LINEN PAPER: MAMBI
RUSTED WIRE: Darice
BELT BUCKLE: 7gypsies
LEATHER LACING: American Tag

THE STUFF OF LIFE
TRANSPARENCY: K & Co.
RUB-ON LETTERS: MM

SCRAPPING MUST HAVES
RIBBON: MAMBI

JUST A LITTLE SOMETHIN'
FONT: Splendid 66

ALMOST 4
RUBBER STAMPS: PSX Design
PAPER: 7gypsies, Karen Foster Design and Rusty Pickle

WELCOME ROXIE
FONT: 2Peas Mister Giggles
RUBBER STAMPS: JudiKins

simply put

What started out as a need for an idea book on how to use vellum has evolved into the most respected idea book series in the scrapbooking industry. Through it all, our books have continued to stay ahead of the trends with a team of the **best and brightest artists,** who have an "anything goes" approach to technique and style.